Generals Die in Bed

A Story from the Trenches

by
Charles Yale Harrison

Annick Press Ltd.
Toronto • New York • Vancouver

Third printing, August 2004

Annick Press Ltd.

We acknowledge the support of the Canada Council for the Arts, the Ontario
Arts Council, and the Government of Canada through the Book Publishing
Industry Development Program (BPIDP) for our publishing activities.

Cover design by Irvin Cheung/iCheung Design.
Cover illustration by Danuta K. Frydrych.
Map, page 4 by Chum McLeod.
Photo credits:
page 30, 90, 116: William Ivor Castle/Canada. Dept. of National
Defence/National Archives of Canada/ PA-001140
Photo page 134: Canada. Dept. of National Defence/National Archives of
Canada/ PA-001021
Photo page 138: Henry Edward Knobel/Canada. Dept. of National
Defence/National Archives of Canada/ PA-000169

Cataloging in Publication Data

Harrison, Charles Yale, 1898-1954.
          Generals die in bed : a story from the trenches

New rev. ed.
ISBN 1-55037-731-0 (bound).-ISBN 1-55037-730-2 (pbk.)

1. World War, 1914-1918—Fiction. I. Title.

PS8515.A7896G4 2002   C813'.52   C2001-903518-7
PR9199.3.H3466G4 2002

Distributed in Canada by:	Published in the U.S.A. by:
Firefly Books Ltd.	Annick Press (U.S.) Ltd.
66 Leek Crescent	Distributed in the U.S.A. by:
Richmond Hill, ON	Firefly Books (U.S.) Inc.
L4B 1H1	P.O. Box 1338, Ellicott Station
	Buffalo, NY 14205

Printed and bound in Canada.

visit us at: **www.annickpress.com**

A **Teacher's Guide** is available that offers a program of classroom
study based on this book. It is available for free at
www.annickpress.com and click on "For Teachers".

To

the bewildered youths—

British, Australian, Canadian, and German—

who were killed in that wood a few miles beyond

Amiens on August 8, 1918,

I DEDICATE THIS BOOK

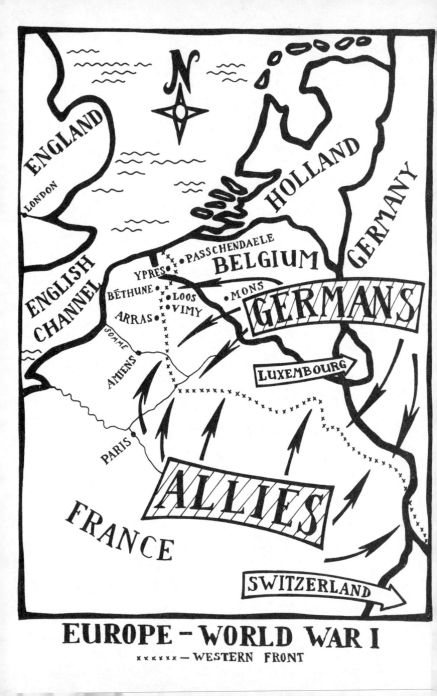

EUROPE – WORLD WAR I
××××× – WESTERN FRONT

CONTENTS

Introduction 6

1. Recruits 13

2. In the Trenches 19

3. Out on Rest 31

4. Back to the Round 41

5. On Rest Again 49

6. Bombardment 63

7. Béthune 91

8. London 103

9. Over the Top 117

10. An Interlude 135

11. Arras 139

12. Vengeance 157

Introduction

On November 11, 1929, the First World War had been over for precisely eleven years. Yet at the top of the best-seller list in the United States was *A Farewell to Arms*, a novel about that war by Ernest Hemingway, an American. Its closest competitor was *All Quiet on the Western Front*, a novel about the same war by Erich Maria Remarque, a German. A swarm of books followed as the men who had fought in the "Great Crusade" described—at last—what it had really been like. One of these books was *Generals Die in Bed* by Charles Yale Harrison, a young American who had served in the Canadian army. It is a shockingly frank portrayal of the experiences of a group of soldiers in the trenches on the Western Front.

The general public was jolted by these books, and mystified that it had taken so long for the soldiers to tell about their experiences. One reason they began to speak up was that the men were frustrated with hearing romantic myths about the war, and wanted people to know the truth. During the war some brave soldiers had decried its horrors in public, but few civilians wanted to believe them.

Right from the beginning of the First World War there was a profound difference between expectation and reality for the average recruit. Up to 1914, war had been popularly regarded as a testing ground, where a young man could exhibit his courage by charging into battle on his trusty steed, brandishing a gleaming sword. In fact, some World War I recruiting posters even showed this image. But now war was different. For the most part the soldiers huddled together in stinking, vermin-infested trenches, hoping not to get blown to bits by an amazing variety of new weaponry. It no longer made any difference how brave you were, because it had no effect on a screaming shell launched by an artillery battery miles away. Suddenly all men were equal; science and technology had neatly eradicated the once profound difference between the hero and the ordinary soldier.

How had all this come about? The origins of the First World War were amazingly complex, but the result would change the world absolutely. Ten million people were killed, most of them young soldiers, who came to be known as "The Lost Generation." The spirit of optimism that had pervaded Europe at the beginning of the war gave way to disillusionment—the world had lost its innocence.

Ironically, it all began with an obscure incident in the tiny country of Serbia, which caused barely a stir in the outside world. Archduke Francis Ferdinand, heir to the Austrian throne, was on a state visit on June 28, 1914, when he and his wife, Sophie, were gunned down by nineteen-year-old Gavrilo Princip, a member of the Serbian "Black Hand." This was the fuse which set off the powder keg that would engulf the world in total war.

Europe was thick with alliances among countries that were filled with patriotic pride, hungry for empire, and bristling with weaponry. Backed by Germany, Austria declared war on Serbia precisely one month after the assassination of the archduke. However, Serbia was supported by Russia, which began to mobilize—so on August 1, Germany declared war on Russia. Now feeling threatened by France, which was eager to regain its provinces of Alsace and Lorraine, Germany declared war against France two days later.

Germany immediately launched an attack on Paris, through Luxembourg and Belgium. Britain had sworn to support Belgium, so the next day, August 4, Britain went to war against Germany. Automatically the countries of the British Empire were involved, and would play a large role in the conflict. Although there were many other nations battling on both sides, the major combatants were "The Allies," or "Triple Entente" (Britain, France, Russia) against "The Central Powers," or "Triple Alliance" (Germany, Austria, and Italy, although Italy joined the Allies in 1915).

The German advance was halted near Paris by the French and British armies at the Battle of the Marne. The Germans retreated and entrenched themselves behind the Aisne River. Within weeks the battle lines were established, and they would remain virtually unchanged until the war ended four years later, on the eleventh hour of the eleventh day of the eleventh month of 1918.

Thus began a "war of attrition," with millions of soldiers

digging two lines in a zigzag system of trenches that stretched for five hundred miles across Europe, from the North Sea to Switzerland. This was the "Western Front," with the area between the opposing forces known as "No Man's Land," an ever-deteriorating sea of mud laced with shell holes, sandbags, barbed wire, corrugated iron—and rotting corpses.

Whereas warfare had once been a matter of one side attacking and the other defending, both forces quickly learned that going "over the top" (leaving the trench to advance) was suicidal. As one side staggered through the mud—or snow or slush—towards the enemy lines, falling into slimy shell holes and getting entangled in coils of barbed wire, the other side mowed them down in rows with machine guns. Yes, war was suddenly very different: instead of rushing into battle, you crouched in a trench and kept your head down (in case it was removed by a sniper) and your mouth shut (to avoid inviting a mortar shell), and prayed for a "Blighty"—a wound that would allow you to return home.

The military brass on both sides quickly adopted the idea that to win the war you simply had to wear down the enemy by hanging in there until he ran out of steam. This was termed "victorious resistance" by the French general Joseph Joffre, while the German general Erich von Falkenhayn called it Stellungskrieg ("position warfare").

Occasionally one side would launch a "major offensive" in an effort to break the stalemate. It would be announced by an intense artillery barrage, to soften up the opposition before running at them. But little or no ground was gained by the attackers. These battles, known by their place names, will live forever as symbols of pointless slaughter: Ypres, Cambrai, Passchendaele, Verdun, the Somme ... During the first day of the Battle of the Somme, 20,000 British soldiers were killed.

Life in the trenches was intolerable and unchanging. The only development was that the enemy employed ever more deadly weapons to eradicate the opposing forces with increasing efficiency. (The German howitzer "Big Bertha" could hurl a shell weighing a ton at a target six miles away.) Added to the fear of death or getting maimed was the threat of frostbite or trench foot or rheumatism or cholera or pneumonia. And there were other, more tangible miseries: the mud and the lice and the rats.

But there was one animal that all participants in the conflict found indispensable. As it had done for centuries, the horse went into battle with man. Although its familiar role as cavalry mount had understandably diminished, it was used to haul field kitchens, supply wagons, and the big guns. A horse could go where trucks could not because of the terrible conditions on the battlefield. Inevitably, thousands of the innocent beasts, large and vulnerable, suffered horribly.

Charles Yale Harrison served with the Canadian Expeditionary Force, which consisted of 600,000 troops. As part of the British Empire, Canada had entered the war in

1914. The Canadians proved themselves early: in 1915, during the Second Battle of Ypres in France, they stood firm when the Germans used poison gas for the first time. Later that year the Canadians suffered 16,000 casualties during the Battle of Passchendaele, fighting in a vast wasteland with mud so deep that soldiers drowned in it. One of the greatest victories of the war was the capture of Vimy Ridge in France in 1917 by the Canadian Corps.

Generals Die in Bed begins in Montreal, Quebec, but almost immediately the reader is whisked to the battlefield. Harrison creates images that communicate vividly the reality of the Western Front. For example, the trees are described as "skeletons holding stubs of stark, shell-amputated arms towards the sky."

Harrison captures the only kind of humor possible under the circumstances—dark and sardonic, a mingling of comedy and horror. (Joseph Heller would use the same humor thirty years later in *Catch-22*, his novel about World War II.) It is seen in *Generals Die in Bed* when American troops arrive in the trenches for the first time. They are bubbling with enthusiasm, shouting smart remarks across No Man's Land, until the fun is abruptly terminated by an artillery bombardment.

This is a significant incident in the novel. It shows how the narrator, acclimatized to the war, fails to identify with his fellow Americans. But more importantly, it signals the entry of the United States into the conflict. Here were fresh troops just when they were needed most: Germany had signed a treaty with Russia and could now send massive reinforcements westward. A declaration of war against Germany by the United States on April 6, 1917, allowed the Allies to erase this inequity.

On June 25, 1917, the first 85,000 men of the American Expeditionary Force arrived in France, commanded by General John "Black Jack" Pershing. Beginning in March 1918, a quarter-million American troops arrived in France each month; by the end of the war there would be two million. On May 28, 1918, the American Expeditionary Force launched its first major offensive, gaining victory at the Battle of Cantigny in northern France. In early June they participated in the second Battle of the Marne, at Belleau Wood near Château-Thierry in France, helping stem the final German offensive.

When *Generals Die in Bed* appeared, it evoked powerful responses. The American novelist John Dos Passos wrote, "*Generals Die in Bed* has a sort of flat-footed straightness about it that gets down the torture of the front line about as accurately as one can ever get it." The *New York Evening Post* dubbed it flat out "the best of the war books."

Robert F. Nielsen
Waterdown, Ontario
November, 2001

Robert Nielsen is a writer, publisher, and instructor of writing at McMaster University in Hamilton, Ontario.

1

Recruits

It is after midnight on payday. Some of the recruits are beginning to dribble into the barracks bunk room after a night's carousal down the line.

"Down the line" in Montreal is Cadieux Street, St. Elizabeth Street, La Gauchetière Street, Vitre Street, Craig Street—a square mile of dilapidated, squalid red brick houses with red lights shining through the transoms, flooding the sidewalks with an inviting, warm glow. The houses are known by their numbers, 169 or 72 or 184.

Some of us are lying in our bunks, uncovered, showing our heavy gray woolen underwear—regulation Army issue.

The heavy odor of stale booze and women is in the air. A few jaundiced electric lights burn here and there in the barn-like bunk room although it is long after "lights out."

In the bunk next to mine lies Anderson, a middle-aged,

slightly bald man. He comes from somewhere in the backwoods of northern Ontario and enlisted a few weeks ago. He was a Methodist lay preacher in civilian life. He is reading his bible. The roistering arrivals annoy him. The conversation is shouted across the bunk room:

"——'three bucks?' I says. 'What the hell! D'yuh know there's a war on? I don't wantta buy yuh,' I says, 'I only want yuh for about twenty minutes.'"

There is a roar of laughter.

"——'I'm thirsty,' I says. 'Where's the water?' When she's gone I dips into her pocketbook and sneaks me two bucks."

A skeptical silence greets this.

"——yeah, that's what you wish had happened."

"Ask Brownie, he heard her bellyachin'—dincha, Brownie?"

A singing, drunken trio bursts through the door of the bunk room and for a moment drowns out the controversy.

A young lad, not more than seventeen, staggers to the center of the room and retches into the slop-can.

Obscene roars from the bunks.

The boy sways.

"Hold it, Billy, hold it."

"Missed it, by God!"

A howl of delight.

The boy staggers back to his bunk. His face is a greenish yellow under the dim lights.

In the far corner of the dormitory some of the boys begin to sing a war song. They sing with a mock pathos.

I don't want to die, I don't want to die,
The bullets they whistle, the cannons they roar,
I don't want to go up the line any more.
Take me over the sea, where Heinie he can't get at me;
Oh, my, I'm too young to die,
I want to go home.

Catcalls and hootings greet the end of the song. There is a silence and then the desultory conversation is resumed. The remarks are addressed to no one in particular. They are hurled into the center of the room and he who wills may reply.

"——hey, lissen, fellers, don't none of you go down to 184 any more; they threw one of our men out tonight."

"Sure, we'll bust her joint up."

I look at Anderson. His forehead is drawn into furrows. He frowns. Little beads of perspiration stand out on his red face. The room is fouled with the odors of dissipation. He waits cautiously for a lull in the conversation. With a spring he jumps into the middle of the room, the seat of the underwear which is too big for him hanging comically in his rear. In an evangelical voice he cries:

"Men, do you know you're sinning in the eyes of the Lord?"

A salvo of oaths greets him.

"Shut up."

"Go to hell."

"Take a jump in the lake."

He is undeterred. He continues:

"Some of you men would put your bodies where I wouldn't put my swagger stick."

"Shut up, sky pilot."

"It's good for pimples."

He stands on the bare floor facing the torrent of ribaldry. His long face is set. His voice sounds like an insistent piccolo above the braying of trombones.

"Well, anyway, God didn't make your bodies for *that*."

He goes back to his bed.

The orderly sergeant crashes through the door and faces us menacingly.

The room is quiet.

*　　　　　*　　　　　*　　　　　*

Our train is to leave Bonaventure Station at eight. At four the officers try to get the men in shape. More than half the battalion is drunk. Pails of black coffee are brought around. Some of the bad ones have buckets of cold water sluiced over them.

It takes an hour to line the men for parade outside the barracks. Men are hauled out of their bunks and strapped into their equipment. They stare vacantly into the faces of those who jostle them.

Outside in the streets we hear the sounds of celebration.

Fireworks are being exploded in our honor.

The drunks are shoved into position.

The officers take their places.

The band strikes up and we march and stagger from the parade square into the street.

Outside a mob cheers and roars.

Women wave their handkerchiefs.

When we come to the corner of St. Catherine and Windsor streets a salvo of fireworks bursts over the marching column. It letters the night in red, white, and blue characters. The pale faces of the swaying men shine under the sputtering lights. Those of us who are sober steady our drunken comrades.

Flowers are tossed into the marching ranks.

Sleek men standing on the broad wide steps of the Windsor Hotel throw packages of cigarettes at us. Drunken, spiked heels crush roses and cigarettes underfoot.

The city has been celebrating the departure of the battalion. All day long the military police had been rounding up our men in saloons, in brothels. We are heroes, and the women are hysterical now that we are leaving. They scream at us:

"Goodbye and good luck, boy-y-y-ys."

They break our ranks and kiss the heavily laden boys. A befurred young woman puts her soft arm around my neck and kisses me. She smells of perfume. After the tense excitement of the day it is delightful. She turns her face to me and laughs. Her eyes are soft. She has been drinking a little. Her fair hair shines from under a black fur toque. I feel lonely. I do not want to go to war. She marches along by my side. The battalion is no longer marching. It straggles, disorganized, down the street leading to the station.

I am only eighteen and I have not had any experiences with women like this. I like this girl's brazenness.

"Kiss me, honey," she commands. I obey. I like all this confusion now. War—heroes—music—the fireworks—this girl's kiss. Nobody notices us. I hang on to her soft furry arm. I cling to it as the station looms at the bottom of the street.

She is the last link between what I am leaving and the war. In a few minutes she will be gone. I am afraid now. I forget all my fine heroic phrases. I do not want to wear these dreadfully heavy boots, nor carry this leaden pack. I want to fling them away and stay with this fair girl who smells faintly of perfume. I grip her arm tightly. I think I could slip away unseen with her. We could run through the crowd, far away somewhere. I remember the taunting song, "*Oh, my, I'm too young to die.*" I am hanging on to her arm.

"Hey, soldier boy, you're hurting my arm."

We are at the station. We are hustled inside. We stagger into the trains. We drop into seats. We wait, for hours, it seems. The train does not move. The singing and cheering outside dies down. In a little while the station is deserted. Only a few lonely baggage men and porters move here and there. At last the train slowly begins to move ...

The boys lie like sacks of potatoes in the red plush-covered seats. Some of us are green under the gills. White-faced, we reel to the toilets. The floor is slimy and wet.

2

In the Trenches

We leave the piles of rubble that was once a little Flemish peasant town and wind our way, in Indian file, up through the muddy communication trench. In the dark we stumble against the sides of the trench and tear our hands and clothing on the bits of embedded barbed wire that runs through the earth here as though it were a geological deposit.

Fry, who is suffering with his feet, keeps slipping into holes and crawling out, all the way up. I can hear him coughing and panting behind me.

I hear him slither into a water-filled hole. It has a green scum on it. Brown and I fish him out.

"I can't go any farther," he wheezes. "Let me lie here, I'll come on later."

We block the narrow trench and the oncoming men stumble on us, banging their equipment and mess-tins on the sides of the ditch. Some trip over us. They curse under their breaths.

Our captain, Clark, pushes his way through the mess. He is an Imperial, an Englishman, and glories in his authority.

"So it's you again," he shouts. "Come on, get up. Cold feet, eh, getting near the line?"

Fry mumbles something indistinctly. I, too, offer an explanation. Clark ignores me.

"Get up, you're holding up the line," he says to Fry.

Fry does not move.

"No wonder we're losing the bloody war," Clark says loudly. The men standing nearby laugh. Encouraged by his success, the captain continues:

"Here, sergeant, stick a bayonet up his behind—that'll make him move." A few of us help Fry to his feet, and somehow we manage to keep him going.

We proceed cautiously, heeding the warnings of those ahead of us. At last we reach our positions.

*   *   *   *

It is midnight when we arrive at our positions. The men we are relieving give us a few instructions and leave quickly, glad to get out.

It is September and the night is warm. Not a sound disturbs the quiet. Somewhere away far to our right we hear the faint sound of continuous thunder. The exertion of the trip up the line has made us sweaty and tired. We slip most of our accouterments off and lean against the parados. We have been warned that the enemy is but a few hundred yards off, so we speak in whispers. It is perfectly still. I remember nights like this in the Laurentians. The harvest moon rides overhead.

Our sergeant, Johnson, appears around the corner of the bay, stealthily like a ghost. He gives us instructions:

"One man up on sentry duty! Keep your gun covered with the rubber sheet! No smoking!"

He hurries on to the next bay. Fry mounts the step and peers into No Man's Land. He is rested now and says that if he can only get a good pair of boots he will be happy. He has taken his boots off and stands in his stockinged feet. He shows us where his heel is cut. His boots do not fit. The sock is wet with blood. He wants to take his turn at sentry duty first so that he can rest later on. We agree.

Cleary and I sit on the firing-step and talk quietly.

"So this is war."

"Quiet."

"Yes, just like the country back home, eh?"

We talk of the trench; how we can make it more comfortable.

We light cigarettes against orders and cup our hands around them to hide the glow. We sit thinking. Fry stands motionless with his steel helmet shoved down almost over his eyes. He leans against the parapet motionless. There is a quiet dignity about his posture. I remember what we were told at the base about falling asleep on sentry duty. I nudge his leg. He grunts.

"Asleep?" I whisper.

"No," he answers, "I'm all right."

"What do you see?"

"Nothing. Wire and posts."

"Tired?"

"I'm all right."

The sergeant reappears after a while. We squinch our cigarettes.

"Everything OK here?"

I nod.

"Look out over there. They got the range on us. Watch out."

We light another cigarette. We continue our aimless talk.

"I wonder what St. Catherine Street looks like—"

"Same old thing, I suppose—stores, whores, theaters—"

"Like to be there just the same—"

"Me too."

We sit and puff our fags for half a minute or so.

I try to imagine what Montreal looks like. The images are murky. All that is unreality. The trench, Cleary, Fry, the moon overhead—this is real.

In his corner of the bay Fry is beginning to move from one foot to another. It is time to relieve him. He steps down and I take his place. I look into the wilderness of posts and wire in front of me.

After a while my eyes begin to water. I see the whole army of wire posts begin to move like a silent host towards me.

I blink my eyes and they halt.

I doze a little and come to with a jerk.

So this is war, I say to myself again for the hundredth time. Down on the firing-step the boys are sitting like dead men. The thunder to the right has died down. There is absolutely no sound.

I try to imagine how an action would start. I try to fancy the preliminary bombardment. I remember all the precautions one has to take to protect one's life. Fall flat on your belly, we had been told time and time again. The shriek of the shell, the instructor in trench warfare said, was no warning because the shell traveled faster than its sound. First, he had said, came the explosion of the shell—then came the shriek and then you hear the firing of the gun ...

From the stories I heard from veterans and from newspaper reports I conjure up a picture of an imaginary action. I see myself getting the Lewis gun in position. I see it spurting darts of flame into the night. I hear the roar of battle. I feel elated. Then I try to fancy the horrors of the battle. I see Cleary, Fry, and Brown stretched out on the firing-step. They are stiff and their faces are white and set in the stillness of death. Only I remain alive.

An inaudible movement in front of me pulls me out of the dream. I look down and see Fry massaging his feet. All is still. The moon sets slowly and everything becomes dark.

The sergeant comes into the bay again and whispers to me:

"Keep your eyes open now—they might come over on a raid now that it's dark. The wire's cut over there—" He points a little to my right.

I stand staring into the darkness. Everything moves rapidly again as I stare. I look away for a moment and the illusion ceases.

Something leaps towards my face.

I jerk back, afraid.

Instinctively I feel for my rifle in the corner of the bay.

It is a rat.

It is as large as a tomcat. It is three feet away from my face and it looks steadily at me with its two staring, beady eyes. It is fat. Its long tapering tail curves away from its padded hindquarters. There is still a little light from the stars and this light shines faintly on its sleek skin. With a darting movement it disappears. I remember with a cold feeling that it was fat, and why.

Cleary taps my shoulder. It is time to be relieved.

*   *   *   *

Over in the German lines I hear quick, sharp reports. Then the red-tailed comets of the *minenwerfer* sail high in the air, making parabolas of red light as they come towards us. They look pretty, like the fireworks when we left Montreal. The sergeant rushes into the bay of the trench, breathless. "Minnies," he shouts, and dashes on.

In that instant there is a terrific roar directly behind us.

The night whistles and flashes red.

The trench rocks and sways.

Mud and earth leap into the air, come down upon us in heaps.

We throw ourselves upon our faces, clawing our nails into the soft earth in the bottom of the trench.

Another!

This one crashes to splinters about twenty feet in front of the bay.

Part of the parapet caves in.

We try to burrow into the ground like frightened rats.

The shattering explosions splinter the air in a million

fragments. I taste salty liquid on my lips. My nose is bleeding from the force of the detonations.

SOS flares go up along our front calling for help from our artillery. The signals sail into the air and explode, giving forth showers of red, white, and blue lights held aloft by a silken parachute.

The sky is lit by hundreds of fancy fireworks like a night carnival.

The air shrieks and catcalls.

Still they come.

I am terrified. I hug the earth, digging my fingers into every crevice, every hole.

A blinding flash and an exploding howl a few feet in front of the trench.

My bowels liquefy.

Acrid smoke bites the throat, parches the mouth. I am beyond mere fright. I am frozen with an insane fear that keeps me cowering in the bottom of the trench. I lie flat on my belly, waiting ...

Suddenly it stops.

The fire lifts and passes over us to the trenches in the rear.

We lie still, unable to move. Fear has robbed us of the power to act. I hear Fry whimpering near me. I crawl over to him with great effort. He is half covered with earth and debris. We begin to dig him out.

To our right they have started to shell the front lines. It is about half a mile away. We do not care. *We are safe.*

Without warning it starts again.

The air screams and howls like an insane woman.

We are getting it in earnest now. Again we throw ourselves face downward on the bottom of the trench and grovel like savages before this demoniac frenzy.

The concussion of the explosions batters against us.

I am knocked breathless.

I recover and hear the roar of the bombardment.

It screams and rages and boils like an angry sea. I feel a prickly sensation behind my eyeballs.

A shell lands with a monster shriek in the next bay. The concussion rolls me over on my back. I see the stars shining serenely above us. Another lands in the same place. Suddenly the stars revolve. I land on my shoulder. I have been tossed into the air.

I begin to pray.

"God—God—please ..."

I remember that I do not believe in God. Insane thoughts race through my brain. I want to catch hold of something, something that will explain this mad fury, this maniacal congealed hatred that pours down on our heads. I can find nothing to console me, nothing to appease my terror. I know that hundreds of men are standing a mile or two from me pulling gun lanyards, blowing us to smithereens. I know that and nothing else.

I begin to cough. The smoke is thick. It rolls in heavy clouds over the trench, blurring the stabbing lights of the explosions.

A shell bursts near the parapet.

Fragments smack the sandbags like a merciless shower of steel hail.

A piece of mud flies into my mouth. It is cool and refreshing. It tastes earthy.

Suddenly it stops again.

I bury my face in the cool, damp earth. I want to weep. But I am too weak and shaken for tears.

We lie still, waiting ...

*   *   *   *

We do not know what day it is. We have lost count. It makes no difference whether it is Sunday or Monday. It is merely another day—a day on which one may die.

The shelling a few nights ago smashed our section of the trench. We built it up again and the next night another shell demolishes it. We are now exposed to rifle fire on our left flank. There are snipers in the woods about half a mile away. All day long we have to crawl on our bellies. Brownie straightened up for a moment when he was going to the latrine yesterday and a sniper knocked his helmet off. He came into the dugout and related his experience to us:

"God, a man can't even pump ship without being shot at. Some war!"

*   *   *   *

We are supposed to be resting, but rest is impossible; we are being eaten alive by lice. We cannot sleep for them. We sit and talk, and dig feverishly in our chests, under our arms, between our legs. Our rambling conversation is interrupted by sharp little cracks as we crush the vermin between our thumbnails.

A tiny drop of blood spurts in one's face as they are crushed.

We talk of our experiences with the *minenwerfer*—the mine-throwing trench mortars—the other night. Cleary speaks up:

"I thought I was dead a dozen times. When that sandbag caught me on the head I thought I was a goner."

I quote: "He who lives more lives than one, more deaths than one must die."

"What's that?"

"A line from one of Wilde's poems."

He looks at me for a moment in silence.

"Aw, crap."

"Who is this guy, Wilde?" Fry asks.

I start to tell him, but the words sound hollow and flat here. I stress the scandalous features of the story and repeat an epigram that once sounded so sparkling in my high-school days. Fry closes his eyes and turns his head away.

I begin to feel down the seam of my trousers for lice.

    *   *   *   *

Tomorrow we are to be relieved. We keep talking about it all day.

We are going insane with scratching. My chest is a raw wound. When I am awake I scratch as little as possible, but when I sleep I scratch until I bleed and the pain wakes me up. Yesterday when I crawled into the dugout after sentry duty, I heard Brown moaning in his sleep and scratching under his arms.

The sapper who was helping us repair the trench the other night said that the Germans brought the lice with them from Germany.

"They are a filthy rice; the bloody swine," he added in a cockney accent.

I suggested that possibly the dirt and the dead bodies might be the cause. He looked at me sharply and said:

"I says they're Heinie lice and I knaow. They got black stripes on their backs, 'aven't they? In Blighty I never saw a louse with black stripes on them. They're bloody bosches. I knaow."

*   *   *   *

On the way down to the latrine yesterday I noticed that a shell had torn a hole into one of the sides of the communication trench. Some wire stuck out from the hole, some old cans of unopened bully beef, and the toe of a boot.

It was an officer's boot made of soft brown leather.

I tugged at it until it gave way a little and then it came easily.

It was filled with a decaying foot. The odor was sickening. I dropped it in disgust.

When I came back, Brown limped towards the latrine. He was gone quite a while; when he returned he had a pair of soft brown leather shoes tucked under his arm.

"I found them near the ——house," he said. "They're dirty, but with a little cleaning they'll be all right. They're just the right size. I tried them on."

He sat down beside me and took his shoe and sock off. "Look at this," he said, showing me his foot. The back of his heel was as raw as a lump of meat.

Canadian soldiers on Main Street, Vimy, France, May 1917

3

Out on Rest

We are out on rest now for the third time. We are in a little peasant village; a score or so of neglected, half-ruined houses and as many barns, pigsties, sheds. The officers occupy a deserted chateau. My section is quartered in a large barn with a gaping roof. Successive battalions have rested here and have used the planks of the roof as fuel. We continue the tradition. In the yard outside is a towering manure pile, sodden with rich plant-nourishing, steaming juices which we smell even in our sleep.

Each man has a pile of ancient gray straw on which he makes his bed. It is so vermin-infested that if one stands and listens when it is quiet he can hear the scraping and scurrying of the pests underneath.

It is late afternoon; we are through with the day's fatigues and are sitting about digging mud off our boots, shining brass buttons, cleaning and oiling our rifles, and killing lice in between times.

We have long since learned that the word *rest* is another military term meaning something altogether different. Take artillery duel, for example. We are in the line—suddenly the enemy artillery begins to bombard us. We cower behind the sandbags, trembling, white-faced, tight-lipped. Our own guns reply. They begin to hammer the enemy's front line. The infantrymen on both sides suffer, are killed, wounded. This is called an artillery duel.

We are taken from the trenches and march for endless hours to billets. The first day out we really rest. Then begins an interminable routine of fatigues. We march, drill, shine buttons, do guard duty, serve as batmen for the officers, practice grenade-throwing, machine gunnery, and at night we are taken by lorry behind the lines to do wiring and trench-digging. This is called out on rest.

Clark, our captain, does not make life any too pleasant for us. He is tall and blond and takes an insufferable pride in his uniform. He wears very light, smart buckskin riding breeches in and out of the trenches. His leather is brightly polished and his equipment and insignia gleam malignantly in contrast with our seedy, mud-stained uniforms. Yesterday he gave us a stern lecture on cleanliness and ordered that we must shave every day. It gives you greater morale, he said. How can you expect to kill a German when you feel like dying yourself? he asked. It is bitter cold, and when we shaved this morning in the cold water our faces were blue for hours afterwards.

*   *   *   *

Today Brownie came under Clark's displeasure. Wherever

there is a stray bit of barbed wire Brown is sure to be hooked onto it. His uniform is almost in tatters. The stuff is shoddy and comes apart easily. Before drill this morning Clark hauled him over the coals for being a disgrace to the company. Brownie stood erect and glared. This infuriated Clark and he ordered Brown's name be taken for "silent insolence."

Brown is now sitting on his pile of straw muttering imprecations at his officer.

"I'll kill the bastard—that's what I'll do. I'm just waiting until we get into a real scrap. I'll plug the son of a bitch between the shoulder blades."

We go on with our scraping and polishing. We are silent in the face of the torrent of oaths and complaints which stream from Brown.

After a while Broadbent, the lance-corporal, begins our favorite game. Between the cracking of lice he says:

"If you had a wish what would you wish for?"

Brown is the first wisher.

"I wish that bloody bastard Clark was dead."

"A lot of good that's gonna do you," says Fry. "That won't put beans in your belly."

"Just the same, I'd give a month's pay to see him stretched out."

"Clean sheets," a voice says from a darkened corner of the barn. It is Cleary. "Great big, white, cool sheets and no lice, and I'm willing to let White Breeches live."

We all agree.

We are filthy, our bodies are the color of the earth we have been living in these past months. We are alive with vermin and sit picking at ourselves like baboons. It is months since we have been out of our clothes. We begin to talk of the last time we slept between sheets. A flood of reminiscences begins. Brown forgets his hatred for Clark for the moment and rhapsodizes over his last night in a real bed.

Brown is a farmer's son. He came from Prince Edward Island. He is tall, awkward, and continually stumbling into things. He does not grasp ideas quickly, not even the simple military ones, and this has made him the butt for the ridicule of his mates and an object of hatred for Clark. He is about the same age as most of us—nineteen or twenty.

He is the only married man in the section. Two weeks before the battalion left Montreal a girl whom he knew back home came to the barracks and they got married. He obtained permission from the colonel to live outside. They took a furnished room somewhere and for two weeks Brown enjoyed complete and absolute married bliss.

We now know every little detail of that honeymoon. While waiting to entrain or lying in dugouts between fatigues, Brown has gradually pieced together for us the brief few days of his married life. He starts to tell us again of his last night with Martha:

"The last night I slept between clean white sheets was with my wife. Oh, man!"

He smiles in contemplation.

We urge him to tell us more. We know the story in all its minute variations, but we egg him on.

It is one of the many ways we can forget the war for a few moments. The joking is raw, cruel, and we know it, but continue nevertheless.

We have heard every physical and emotional foible of Martha's. It seems as though we are all married to her. We know, as well as Brown does, that she has a large mole on her right thigh near her hip; he has told us of all her reactions to his advances on the marital night. We enjoy these confidences like the moujik who, when he could have no vodka, preferred talking about it.

Anderson, the ex-lay preacher, is with us. His wish is that the war would end, but this is against the rules of the game. The wish must be specific. His is ruled out.

"I wish I was home with Martha," says Brown.

The wishing is resumed. It begins in earnest when someone wishes for food.

Cleary speaks:

"What's the use of wishing for weeks in bed with a fat wench. Why, Brownie, you'd cave in after the first ten minutes. We haven't had a decent meal for months. I mean a meal. I'd give everything I own for a big helping of English roast beef, red inside and tapering off to a crisp brown outside—big brown baked potatoes split open on top and sprinkled with a little paprika—and a great hunk of Yorkshire pudding. Top that off with a bottle of cool ale."

He sucks his saliva loudly and closes his eyes. After a while he adds: "And by roast beef I mean beef and not horses' meat—it's gotta be soft, juicy, and red with a little blood oozing out of it."

"And to think," says Fry, "of all the good meals I turned down in my life. Many's the time I passed up a big dish of brown beef stew with red carrots and yellow turnips floating in it, just to run out and grab a ham sandwich in a restaurant. If I ever get out of this, I'll never refuse a thing my mother sets before me."

"What's the matter with a ham sandwich?" Broadbent asks.

"And to think that I once told the old lady that roast goose was too rich for me and turkey was too dry. I can see that goose now, stuffed with apples and chestnuts and little rivers of fat running down the sides."

It is Broadbent's turn:

"The best meal I ever had was when I got my five days' leave in London. A tart took me to a place in Soho. Man, I put it away until I thought I would bust. You know, I think that soldiering makes your belly shrink—"

At this we lapse into silence.

We are hungry.

It is four o'clock and it is a full hour before we will get our hunk of gray war bread dipped in bacon grease and a mess-tin full of pale unsweetened tea.

*   *   *   *

We have learned who our enemies are—the lice, some of our officers, and Death.

Of the first two we speak continually, the last we rarely refer to.

Strangely, we never refer to the Germans as our enemy. In

the week-old newspaper which comes up from the base we read of the enemy and the Hun, but this is newspaper talk and we place no stock in it. Instead we call him Heinie and Fritz. The nearest we get to unfriendliness is when we call him "square-head." But our persistent and ever present foe is the louse.

We have been sleeping in our clothes now for months. It is impossible to take them off. It is winter and the barn is cold. We have rigged up a stove of sorts made of some piping and tin which we found nearby. We sit facing the fire and talk in a rambling fashion. As we talk we hunt for lice.

Fry suddenly appears at the door with a flatiron in his hand.

"What's that for?" Broadbent asks.

"The goddamned lice," Fry grunts.

"What are you going to do? Brain 'em?"

"You just watch."

He takes a board and places his tunic on the board. We watch closely. He heats the iron over the fire and then runs the hot iron down the seam. There is a quick series of cracks. Little spurts of blood come in a stream from the inside of the seam. Fry looks up triumphantly.

"That's the way to kill 'em, by God. And it kills the eggs, too."

We all take our tunics and trousers off and begin to iron the lice out of our clothes.

"How about the straw?" Anderson asks. "It's alive."

We see that this will be an endless game.

"Anyway," says Fry, "we'll sleep tonight for a couple of hours."

Johnson, the sergeant, appears at the door.

"Brown," he says, "orderly room for you."

Brown puts on his tunic and puttees and we look him over to see that he is properly dressed for his appearance before the colonel. He goes out.

In the meantime our food comes around—a hunk of bread the size of a fist, a piece of cheese, a raw onion, and a mess-tin full of unsweetened tea.

We are smoking after supper and Brown reappears.

"What d'yuh get?" we ask.

"Two hours pack drill," he answers and sits down to eat. We have nothing to say, so we sit by quietly as he munches his food.

*   *   *   *

In a field beyond the few houses and barns which form the village is the parade ground. It is nearly dark. Out of the twilight heavily laden forms emerge. The earth is soft and soggy. Brown, like the others, is ready for his pack drill. He is dressed in his greatcoat, carries full equipment and pack, rifle, and one hundred and twenty rounds of ammunition in his pouches. Johnson, the sergeant, is in charge. He inspects each man; there are about ten.

Fry and I stand nearby and watch.

"Squad, ten-shun!"

Twenty heels smack together.

Johnson is not satisfied.

"Now, then, smarter than that! As you were!"

The men relax.

He repeats the order.

Again and again.

Finally he gives the order to march. It is growing darker.

"On the double."

The men begin to trot. Their equipment rattles and bangs. The men in the rear begin to lag.

"Get it right now, youse guys in the rear. We'll stay here all night if you don't snap into it."

Around and around they trot, clanging and banging. The mud is squishy and sticks to the boots of the trotters.

Fry mutters under his breath. "Come on, let's go. I can't bear to see it."

The running, grotesque squad passes us. We hear their panting and wheezing. Even in the half-dark we can see the red, strained faces, the wide-opened eyes.

We can stand it no longer: we know the agony of the jumping pack, the banging of the entrenching tools on the buttocks, the leaden ammunition tugging at aching shoulders. We walk away towards the *estaminet*.

As we walk we hear Johnson shout: "Come on, make it snappy," and we hear a slight acceleration of the clanging of the drillers' equipment.

"That's the hell of it," says Fry. "Eighteen days in the line, get the guts shelled out of yuh—and then all the thanks yuh get is this—" He jerks his thumb towards the parade ground.

We enter the *estaminet*. The warm sour odor of wine fills

our nostrils. Voices, cheered by wine, call to us. We sit down at a table. The madame, red-faced, mountainous bosom, beady eyes, serves us with a bottle of *vin rouge*.

"He'll be too damned tired to come down here after he's done," Fry says.

The heat, the wine, goes to our heads. We feel that we ought to do something for poor Brownie, but we cannot think of anything.

This is war; there is so much misery, heartaches, agony, and nothing can be done about it. Better to sit here and drink the sour, hard wine and try to forget. The blue haze of tobacco smoke begins to sway a little.

Better to forget ...

But it is not easy to forget. Fry's wine makes him talkative, moody, bitter. His face wears an ugly expression of half sneer, half scowl.

"They take everything from us: our lives, our blood, our hearts; even the few lousy hours of rest, they take those, too. Our job is to give, and theirs is to take ..."

We order another bottle.

4

Back to the Round

Six days in reserve near the light artillery, six days in supports, six days in the front trenches—and then out to rest. Five or six days out on rest and then back again; six days, six days, rest.

Endlessly in and out. Different sectors, different names of trenches, different trenches, but always the same trenches, the same yellow, infested earth, the same screaming shells, the same comet-tailed "minnies" with their splintering roar. The same rats, fat and sleek with their corpse-filled bellies, the same gleaming gimlet eyes. The same lice which we carry with us wherever we go. In and out, in and out, endlessly, sweating, endlessly, endlessly ... Somewhere it is summer, but here are the same trenches. The trees here are skeletons holding stubs of stark, shell-amputated arms towards the sky. No flowers grow in this waste land.

This is our fifth day in the front line, one more day and out we go back to rest.

For the past few days it has been raining ceaselessly. We are soaked and chilled.

It is near dawn.

As the smudge of gray appears in the east, the odors of the trenches rise in a miasmal mist on all sides of us. The soaked earth here is nothing but a thin covering for the putrescence which lies underneath; it smells like a city garbage dump in mid-August. We are sunk in that misery which men fall into through utter hopelessness.

We are in a shallow trench and last night the enemy trench mortars blew away part of the parapet, so that now we are exposed to enfilade fire from our left.

We will have to wait until nightfall to repair it.

They are sniping at us.

About two hundred yards from us there is a little wood, and in this wood there are snipers hidden somewhere among the trees.

The broken parapet does not hide us and we have to crawl around on our hands and knees because the sniper can shoot *down the length of our trench.*

We remember what the instructor in trench warfare told us at the base. "Enfilade fire is fire directed down the length of a line or trench. It is fire coming from the flanks. Keep low."

But the instructor is at the base, safe and comfortable, and we are here in this muddy trench.

Six short days in a trench!

It is nothing, it seems; less than a week, but it seems like an eternity as we wait for night when we shall be relieved.

The dugouts here are filled with water and we live in hastily constructed funk-holes, holes burrowed into the side of the parapet or parados. We are wet to the skin.

Why do we crawl about here?

It would be better, it seems, to dash into No Man's Land and chance death, or down the communication trench to temporary safety—and a firing squad. But we are disciplined. Months of training on the rolling Sussex downs, at the base, in the periods of rest, have stiffened us. We must carry on, carry on ...

In a thousand ways this has been drilled into our heads. The salute, the shining of our brass buttons, the correct way to twist a puttee, and so on. A thousand thundering orders! A thousand trivial rules, each with a penalty for an infraction, has made will-less robots of us all. All, without exception ...

Half a mile from our partly exposed trench, hidden in the hollow of a tree, sits a sniper holding an oiled, perfect rifle.

Every night they bring him his rations, maybe with a little extra schnapps, for I know our snipers get an extra rum ration.

Sooner or later this German sniper, who keeps us cowering in cold fear, will be caught in an advance by our troops.

We will fall upon him and bayonet him like a hapless trench rat. He will crawl out of his hiding place as the first wave swarms about him menacingly. He will hold his trembling hands on high and stammer the international word for compassion and mercy. He will say that beautiful word *comrade*, a word born in suffering and sorrow, but we will stab him down shouting to one another, "Hey, look, we found a sniper!" And our faces will harden, our inflamed eyes will become slits, and men will stab futilely at his prostrate body.

But now they bring him his little extra rations.

His rifle is fitted with telescopic sights so that we are brought quite close to him. Slowly he elevates his weapon, looks through the glass, and sees his target as though it is but a few feet away. Then he pulls the trigger and one of us drops out of sight.

In our shattered trench we move about almost doubled over in two, much as a man does who is suffering with abdominal pains. Sometimes to get relief we crawl, like babies, on all fours.

The sniper's rifle cracks and we flop down groveling in the muddy bottom of the trench. Minutes pass before we move. No one is dead and slowly we face each other with gray, sheepishly smiling faces.

We lie cowering in the bottom of the trench.

There is nothing to do until rations come up, and we talk in whispers.

It is graying in the east.

The war sleeps.

No guns.

The machine-gunners are quiet.

We talk.

"You'd think a guy would like to die living a life like this," says Fry. "But we flop just the same."

"How do you know you're gonna get killed for sure?" says Brown.

Anderson does not speak, he lies with his cheek glued to the ground. His lips move in prayer. He gives us the creeps.

"Maybe you'd only go blind or go batty or something."

"Yeah, that's it. How do you know you're gonna get killed?"

We all agree that a swift death would be a pleasant thing. At the crack of the distant rifle we cower lower in silent fear.

It is dawn now.

Soon a carrier will bring us our rations, and as soon as it is divided between us and we have filled our bellies, we will go to sleep and leave one man on sentry duty.

It is quiet. The guns are quiet. Even the sniper is quiet. It is half an hour since last his rifle sent us flopping into the mud.

Over the trench a few sparrows squabble and chirp with carefree energy. They swoop down on the sandbagged parapet and sit looking at us with perky heads cocked to one side.

We look at them in amazement.

They startle us with their noisy merriment, these foolish birds who may live in peaceful fields and forests and who come to look for food on a barren, waste battlefield.

They fly away suddenly towards the German lines.

"They're lost, I guess," Brown says.

The ration carrier crawls round the corner of the bay of the trench and dumps a hairy sandbag half filled with grub on the firing-step. He says nothing and walks away. He is tired; he has been carrying food all night.

We take turns in sharing the food among ourselves. Today it is Brown's turn.

He spreads his rubber sheet along the firing-step. He bends low and empties the food into the sheet; a piece of yellow cheese, three large Spanish onions, a paper container of Australian jam labeled strawberry, but made of figs and artificially flavored with chemicals which we can taste but do not mind; some tea, sugar, condensed milk, and a great hunk of gray war bread.

With hungry, grimy fingers he deftly cuts, slices, divides the food. We look on with greedy, alert eyes to see that justice is being done. From time to time he looks nervously over his shoulder in the direction of the concealed sniper in the distant woods. Our eyes follow his. His glance catches mine and he smiles faintly.

"Don't want to die before breakfast, eh?" he says.

I smile and nod and look at the food.

Anderson stands up to get a better view of the food. He leans over my shoulder.

Broadbent snarls a warning.

We are nervous.

The grub is soon divided into five equal parts. We each take our share and stuff it into our haversacks. We will eat it at leisure in the funk-hole after stand-down. The sun will soon rise and the immediate danger of an attack will be over.

Brown shakes the rubber sheet clean of bread crumbs and bits of onion skin.

Now he will divide the sugar. Precious sugar with which we will sweeten the strong, hot tea that comes up at midnight in large Thermos cans. Tea so bitter that it curls one's tongue. Strong tea, alive with tannic acid to soothe frayed, trench-shattered nerves, tea to still a thumping heart. Sugar to make it palatable. We watch him in silence.

The rusty spoon for dishing out sugar and such things is stuck between two sandbags in the parapet over his head.

Glad to straighten himself up for a second, Brown stands up to reach for it.

He turns to look in the direction of the woods to his left.

In that instant his head snaps back viciously from the impact of the bullet.

The report of the rifle fills our ears like the sound of a cannon.

He sags to the bottom of the sloppy trench.

His neck is twisted at a foolish, impossible angle.

Between his eyes, a little over the bridge of his nose, is a small neat hole. A thin, red stream runs from it.

No one moves.

On the parados to the rear of us a bit of slimy gray matter jiggles as it sticks to the hairy sacking of the sandbag.

At the crack of the sniper's rifle we crouched lower in the trench and looked with stupid amazement as Brown's body fell clumsily into our midst.

We look without resentment towards the woods. We are animated only by a biting hunger for safety. Safety ...

The sun is rising slowly now, it throws a pink pearly light on the parados behind us and colors the motionless bit of Brown's brains.

Everything is quiet.

It is stand-down along the whole front.

The sun warms us a little. We look towards the east, towards the German lines from whence came the swift bullet that had thrown Brown's body awkwardly among us; we look towards the east where the rising sun now slowly begins to climb into the heavens ...

We pull the heavy, limp body out of the mud. Its neck is twisted in such a manner that it seems to be asking a question of us.

We lay it on the firing-step and cover it with a gray woolen, regulation blanket. The blanket is short; it hides the head but reaches only to the ankles. The muddy boots stick out in V-formation.

The sugar is not yet divided. Some of it is spilled and dissolved in the bottom of the trench. Broadbent salvages as much of it as he can. Dispensing with the spoon, he uses his hands. He scoops the remaining sugar into four instead of five parts.

Soon a stretcher-bearer will come and take the body down to company headquarters. Broadbent takes the bread and cheese out of Brown's haversack and shares it with us.

"Anyway," he explains, "he can't eat any more ..."

5

On Rest Again

We are relieved. Down the long, winding communication trenches and at last out onto the open field. It is shortly after midnight, and we straggle past belching light field artillery and silhouetted, silent waiting tanks.

We reach a road.

We are ordered to fall in.

Horse- and tractor-drawn guns, monster swaying supply-lorries roar, chug, and clatter on the cobble-paved road.

The horses strain at their harness.

Chains clank.

The enemy knows that here is a crossroad.

He knows that the road is alive with troops and traffic at this hour. He sprays the road with overhead shrapnel.

Whiz-z-z-z. Cr-r-r-ung.

A long-drawn-out hiss and wail and then a vicious, snarling explosion overhead. The dark is stabbed with a burst of red flame. We duck our heads and hunch our shoulders instinctively.

Instantly there is confusion everywhere. The drivers yell furiously at the animals. The chauffeurs grind their gears into high speed.

More red stabs into the blackness over our heads.

They come faster and faster.

The air whines.

One bursts directly over us. The metal balls rattle on the cobblestones in front of us.

We take to the fields.

But the vehicles must stay on the road. A lorry gets stuck and blocks the road. Whips snap like revolver shots over the heads of the struggling beasts. The horses rear on their hind legs, their mouths drip white flaky foam. Their eyes are distended like those of frightened women. The drivers crack their whips, calling them foul names. We ask one another why we must wait here under this fire.

No one knows.

The rain of steel continues.

A horse is wounded.

We hear the beast's shriek above the howl of the bombardment. It is one of the four horses drawing a light field-piece. The wounded animal whirls around, dragging his mute, pawing mates with him. The team careers for a moment and crashes into the stalled lorry.

A shell bursts over the lorry.

The driver is hurled from his seat.

He is wounded. His cries mingle with the piteous shrieking of the wounded horses.

Two animals are now prone and the other two tear at the harness and kick wildly at the cannon.

Two stretcher-bearers appear and try to extricate the lorry-driver, who is being kicked to death by the frantic horses.

The road is an inferno.

The fire subsides.

We hear the explosions on another road to our left ...

We are ordered to fall in. Four men in our company are wounded. They are carried away to the field dressing station nearby. We begin our trek towards billets.

We march for hours.

Down dark shell-torn roads, past ruined, gutted corpses of houses which once sheltered peaceful peasant families here. We march at a quick pace even though we are unutterably tired. Where are we going? we wonder.

We have been marching for two hours. The stately poplars which line the road here are less scarred. Here and there we see a peasant's house which is not destroyed. We see a faint light showing from behind the tightly drawn blinds. People live here! Our set faces relax. We look at one another and smile wanly.

At last we come to a narrow-gauge railhead. It is still dark. We are ordered to halt. The heat of our exhausted bodies loosens the foul trench odors which cling to us. We throw ourselves panting onto the softness of a bordering field.

It is strangely quiet. Only in the distance do we hear the rumbling of massed artillery fire. We never escape this ominous thunder. It is the link which binds us to our future.

Out on rest, miles behind the lines, we hear it. It is a reminder to us that the line is still there; that we must return. We lie prostrate, still ...

Nearby the tiny narrow-gauge engine puffs energetically, giving off little clouds of white feathery steam which float slowly over us. We look about us with hungry eyes.

Smoke that is not the harbinger of death!

A field which is not the hiding place of thousands of men lurking in trenches to tear each other apart!

The dark, silent, brooding sky above us which does not pour shrieking, living steel upon our heads ...!

Cleary rolls closer to me, he talks.

"Smell it?"

I nod.

We are lying near a field of blossoming beans. The air is filled with the heavy fragrance. We take deep, long inhalations. Our bodies are cooling and the foul trench odors cease stirring. We hear the buzzing and humming of nocturnal insects. Here is life. Fragrant, peaceful life ...The scent of the blossoms beats on us in waves, undulating.

I lie on my back. I look at the stars. We talk quietly as though fearful of disturbing this restful silence.

"What is it?"

"Beans."

"Beans?"

"Yes, beans; they smell like this when they are in blossom."

"Jeez, I thought beans ..." He makes a crude joke about beans, an Army joke.

"It's a shame about Brownie."

"Yes."

"Maybe ..."

"Yeah, I suppose so—better out of it."

Fry rolls over to where we are lying and joins in the conversation.

"Private?"

"Naw. Free for all."

"Just sayin' about Brownie."

"Tough."

"Aw, I don't know. Better out of it."

"D'you smell it, Fry?"

"Yes, what is it?"

"Beans."

"I thought beans only—" Again the same joke. A soldier's joke—a joke born of bitterness and suffering. A joke to dispel horror. A joke to make one weep.

"Yeah, they smell like this when they're in blossom."

"It's a shame about Brownie. He'd love this. Always talking about potatoes and beans and how he hoed 'em. Remember how he told that frog farmer how to dig his spuds?"

"Yeah, he came from Prince Edward Island."

"Prince Edward Island potatoes. Used to see them back home in the markets."

"Well, now he's pushin' them up."

"He sure liked to talk about farming."

"Remember Martha?"

"Gee, I was sorry I kidded him about her."

"It used to get under his skin."

We speak respectfully of Brown now. He is dead. He is not the awkward, stupid boy we knew. He is a symbol. He is a dead farmer. Martha is a widow now because of his death.

We become silent and lie on our backs waiting for the order to fall in.

     *   *   *   *

We clamber into the toylike open cars. We are jammed tight. We wait for hours, it seems, until the train begins to start.

Through wide fields, through sleeping little villages, past dark woods we go. We lean against the rattling sides. We begin to nod with the monotonous rocking of the train. On and on! We know we are going for a long rest. On and on we go, racing away from the front, back towards peace, quiet, human voices ... No shells, no trenches. The rattling of the wheels takes up the thought. No shells, no trenches, no shells, no trenches ...

We wake up.

The train has come to a stop.

It is dawn.

We stumble out of the cars and line up along the track. We are near a large village. We are detailed off into sections and marched away to billets.

The guide for our section takes us to a large barn. We remove our equipment and fling ourselves down to sleep.

It is afternoon when we wake. We begin to look for water and the toilets. We find out where the cookhouse is. We start to make the barn more livable. Rumors are afloat that we will rest here for two weeks.

One man says that he heard a captain say to a sergeant that we are out for a month.

Fry has been up for some time. He comes into the sunlit entrance of the barn full of information.

"It's payday. You can get good cognac here for five francs a bottle. We're here for a month. It's a big village. I saw three good-looking tarts."

He utters the information breathlessly.

We pelt him with questions.

We jump up and begin to dress.

We run with our mess-tins to the cookhouse.

On the way we hear all sorts of rumors again. As we wait in line before the field kitchens we talk.

"... two months."

"How d'you know?"

"Sergeant told me."

"Aw ..."

"Ask him ..."

"Big scrap. Gonna fatten us up. Two months' rest. See, they're givin' us real bacon. Sugar in the coffee."

"Aw, latrine rumors!"

*   *   *   *

We line up in alphabetical order before the paymaster. We present our little brown pay books, he makes an entry, and gives us a few crisp notes. We salute and walk away gleefully.

Pay. Cognac, eggs and chips, wine, sardines, canned peaches, biscuits. Fry said there were some good-looking Janes in this town. It is six o'clock.

Fry meets me and we start off towards the *estaminet* together.

"I'm gonna eat until my belly begins to creak."

"Me, too."

We enter the *estaminet*. The familiar odor of warm sour wine strikes us. We order six eggs apiece, a mountain of browned potato chips, a bottle of wine each. The hefty madame serves us silently.

We fall to without speaking. We wolf our food. We swallow glasses of wine. The room is full of hungry soldiers. We wipe the yellow bottoms of our plates with chunks of bread and sit back contented, at last.

The wine has warmed our insides.

Fry shouts to the madame. "Hey, madame, *encore, encore* ..."

He points to his empty bottle. Two more bottles are put before us. We drink slowly now, rolling the sharp wine under our tongues.

We get up after a while. We stagger slightly. In the corner of the room a crap game is in progress. We try our luck for a couple of minutes, and when we have lost ten francs each we go back to our table. We order another bottle of wine.

Fry becomes moody. His voice is thick with wine. I, too, am a little groggy. It is a fine, forgetful feeling. The fat madame behind her counter seems more sullen. She sways a little, it seems. The room is a bedlam. In the corner where the crap game is going on, the shouts become louder and louder. Fry puts his hand in his pocket and counts the money.

"Ten francs. C'mon, let's get another bottle of *rouge*."

I agree.

We go to the counter and order a quart of red wine and a bottle of cognac. We take the bottles and stagger out into the street. Men are roaring down the street. There is no light save from the moon. We hear the whirr of an airplane motor high over our heads. Fry carries the wine, I the cognac.

I suggest that we take the liquor to the barn and that we drink it there. We start down the street towards our billets. Others are walking in our direction. A pair of girls walk in front of us. Fry feels gay and shouts the few French phrases he knows:

"Hey, *mam'selle, voulez-vous coucher avec moi ce soir?*"

The girls giggle. They are youngsters about sixteen or so. They still wear their hair in plaits down their backs. They do not quicken their paces. That's a good sign.

Encouraged, Fry sings to them. There is a note of bitterness in his hilarity:

Après la guerre finis, et les soldats parti,
Mademoiselle in the family way,
Après la guerre finis.

The girls turn a corner and run down a side street.

"What the hell would they be wanting with us?" he says, "with all the damned one-pips* around. C'mon, let's finish the stuff here."

We walk on a bit until we reach an open field. We draw

---

*Lieutenants.

the cork of the bottle of cognac and take long swigs from it.

In between whiles we tell sentimental stories of our lives to each other.

Gradually we grow incoherent.

The houses nearby begin to spin around.

I lie down in the cool grass ...

I feel a jab in my back. I look up. It is an MP.

"C'mon, c'mon, back to billets."

I am still groggy. I waken Fry.

We struggle to our feet.

He stares at me stupidly, blinking his eyes like a rooster. We start off down the road, back to our billets. Our unsteady heavy footsteps echo in the silent street.

Over our shoulders we hear the faint thunder of the line.

*   *   *   *

The inhabitants of the town are wretched creatures. Their houses are quartered with officers and non-coms. We sleep in their barns. Their men are at the front and many fields lie fallow. There is a shortage of food and most of the women and girls are thin, scraggy objects. The only fleshy person in the whole place is madame of the *estaminet*.

It is after drill in the afternoon. Cleary is sitting beside me oiling his rifle.

"Get any yet?"

"What?"

"Tarts?"

"Scraggy-looking crew," I reply.

"Any port in a storm."

He leans over towards me and tells me the important secret of the town.

"... so I'm walking down past battalion headquarters and there's a little French tart, a little thin but a bit of all right, just the same. Kind of lively eyes, big like. *Voulez-vous coucher*, I says, and she *oui-oui*'s me. She takes me down to her mother's place and we go into a shed. '*Combien*,' I says to her as we go in. 'Bully bif,' she says. Can you imagine that—for a tin of bully beef. Man, I'll bet there'll be a run on the quartermaster's stores."

Anderson has been listening in. He gives Cleary a withering look.

"Godless swine, these frogs. No morals. Small wonder that their country is laid in ruins."

"... aw, shut up, Anderson. Well, anyway, I gives her the soldier's farewell."

      *   *   *   *

The afternoons are pleasant. We walk in twos and threes out into the woods. Some of us lie beneath trees smoking, soaking in every peaceful minute. The food is good and there is lots of it. We have been here ten days now. Payday is long since past and we have recovered from our riotous pay night. There is no money among us and we smoke the biting ration cigarettes.

A rumor has it that we are to go in the line in a few days. A motor car from divisional headquarters was parked in front of battalion headquarters all morning. That is bad.

We enjoy the last few days with all our might. Soon we will go back in the line and there are persistent rumors of an offensive.

To the north the cannonading has been furious the last few nights. Last night the walls of the barn shook slightly with the force of the distant bombardment.

The insistent rumble woke me and I walked out into the open. Up towards Belgium the sky flashed like the aurora borealis. Our food has been too good.

We are being fattened for the slaughter.

  *   *   *   *

It is warm and Fry has discovered a little stream about three kilometers from the village. We decide to go swimming. About ten of us set off across the fields. It is late afternoon and the sun slants down upon us as we shout and laugh.

We have nearly lost that aged, harassed look which we wear when we are in the line. We are youngsters again. Most of us are under twenty. Anderson is the only matured man among us. He is forty.

We reach the little river. It is lined with tall bushes and here we tear off our uniforms. Broadbent is the first to undress and plunges into the water with a loud splash, the kind known to boys as a bellywopper. His body is fair and lithe.

During the long winter months in the line, bodies did not exist for us. We were men in uniform; clumsy, bundled, heavy uniforms. It is amazing now to see that we have slim, hard, graceful bodies. Our faces are tanned and weather-beaten and that aged look which the trench gives us still lingers a bit, but our bodies are the bodies of boys.

We plunge naked into the clear water, splashing about and shouting to each other. Only Anderson does not undress fully. He wears his heavy gray regulation underwear. We tease him. He walks gingerly to the water's edge and pokes a toe into the stream. Fry creeps up behind him and shoves him splash into the water. We shout and yell and come to his rescue, dragging him to the bank. Broadbent starts to undo his underwear.

"Come on, Anderson, let's see your body. We know you're a boy," he says in baby fashion.

Anderson fumes, sputters, and strikes out. His face is red and he shouts deadly threats. We laugh and leap into the water.

We duck one another and throw water into each other's faces. A few lads from the village stand on the bank and look at us in silence. They have the faces of little old men. We motion to them to join us but they shake their heads gravely.

Who can describe the few moments of peace and sunshine in a solder's life? The animal pleasure in feeling the sun on a naked body. The cool, caressing, lapping water. The feeling of security, of deep inward happiness ...

In the distance the rumble of the guns is faint but persistent like the subdued throbbing of violins in a symphony. I am still here, it says. You may sleep quietly at night in sweet-smelling hay, you may lie sweating under a tree after drill and marvel at the fine tracings on a trembling leaf over your head, but I am here and you must come back to my howling madness, to my senseless volcanic fury. I am the link that binds you to your future, it mutters.

But the water is cool and inviting and the afternoon grows older. The stream gurgles and swishes against the bank on which we stand. I shake the thought of the guns from my mind.

About a hundred yards up towards the line there is a bend in the stream. "Let's race to the bend and back," Fry shouts. "The last man back buys the wine tonight."

We dive into the water and start upstream. Cleary comes to the surface last but turns and quickly swims towards the bank again.

He stands on the bank and calls us out of the water in a strange voice. He points to the water nearby.

We clamber out and crowd near him. We follow his pointing finger with our eyes. There is something dark in the water near the bank.

It is a dead body. It is wearing the field blue French uniform. We see the thin red stripe wriggling up the trouser leg. An underwater growth has caught a bit of the uniform and the body sways to and fro, moved by the current. In the water it looks bloated and enormous.

Our day is spoiled by this lonely dead soldier, carried to us from the front by the sparkling, sunlit water of the Somme.

We do not say anything to each other. We dry ourselves on our underwear and start to dress.

He is different, this Frenchman, from the hundreds of corpses we have seen in the line. We thought we were safe. We thought we could forget the horrors of the line for a brief few weeks—and here this swollen reminder drifts from the battlefield to spoil a sunny afternoon for us ...

6

Bombardment

We are back in the line.

This is a noisy front. It is in constant turmoil. There is no rest. The enemy rains an endless storm of fire upon us. At night the wire is hammered by the artillery and we live in perpetual fear of raids.

There is talk of an offensive.

Out on rest we behaved like human beings; here we are merely soldiers. We know what soldiering means. It means saving your own skin and getting a bellyful as often as possible ... that and nothing else.

Camaraderie—esprit de corps—good fellowship—these are words for journalists to use, not for us. Here in the line they do not exist.

We fight among ourselves.

The morning rations come up. The food is spread out on the rubber sheet and we start to divide it among ourselves. Bread, the most coveted of all the food, is the bone of contention today. Cleary is sharing it out.

Broadbent suspects that his piece is smaller than the rest.

An oath is spat out.

Cleary replies.

In a moment they are at each other's throats like hungry, snarling animals.

They strike at each other with their fists, they kick with their heavy boots. We intervene, tear them apart, and push them into separate corners of the dugout. Blood streams from Cleary's cheek. Broadbent is alive with hate, white with passion.

"You bloody rat."

"Aw, shut up, Broadbent. Leave him be."

"Who's a rat?"

"You."

"Come on, come on, cut it out."

"Any man that'll steal another man's bread ..."

They rush at each other again. Again we pull them apart.

Cleary wipes the blood from his face. He scowls and holds his hunk of bread in his hands like an animal. Then slowly he begins to gnaw at it.

*   *   *   *

We never become accustomed to the shellfire. Its terror for us increases with each passing day. The days out on rest ease our harried nerves, but as soon as we are back in the line again we are as fearful and jumpy as the newest recruit. With the first hiss and roar of a shell we become terror-stricken as of old.

We look at each other with anxious, frightened faces.

Our lips tighten.

Our eyes open wide.

We do not talk.

What is there to say?

*   *   *   *

Talk of the coming offensive continues.

The sector becomes more tumultuous.

The guns rage all night.

We "stand to" long before dawn and wait at the parapets expecting an attack until long after sunrise.

The fatigues are innumerable.

Every night there are wiring parties, sapping parties, carrying parties. We come back exhausted from these trips. We throw ourselves down in the dugouts for an hour's sleep.

But we do not rest.

There is no time for rest. We stagger around like drunken, forsaken men. Life has become an insane dream.

Sleep, sleep—if only we could sleep.

Our faces become gray. Each face is a different shade of gray. Some are chalk-colored, some with a greenish tint, some yellow. But all of us are pallid with fear and fatigue.

It is three in the morning.

Our section is just back from a wiring party.

The guns are quiet.

Dawn is a short while off ...

We sit on the damp floor of the dugout.

We have one candle between us and around this we sit chewing at the remains of the day's rations.

Suddenly the bombardment begins.

The shells begin to hammer the trench above.

The candlelight flickers.

We look at each other apprehensively. We try to talk as though the thing we dread most is not happening.

The sergeant stumbles down the steps and warns us to keep our battle equipment on.

The dugout is an old German one; it is braced by stout wooden beams. We look anxiously at the ceiling of the hole in which we sit.

The walls of the dugout tremble with each crashing explosion.

The air outside whistles with the rush of the oncoming shells.

The German gunners are "feeling" for our front line.

The crashing of the shells comes closer and closer. Our ears are attuned to the nuances of a bombardment. We have learned to identify each sound.

They are landing on the parapet and in the trench itself now.

We do not think of the poor sentry, a new arrival, whom we have left on lookout duty.

We crowd closer to the flickering candle.

Upstairs the trench rings with a gigantic crack as each shell lands. An insane god is pounding it with Cyclopean fists, madly, incessantly.

We sit like prehistoric men within the ring of flickering light which the candle casts. We look at each other silently.

A shell shatters itself to fragments near the entrance of the dugout.

The candle is snuffed out by the concussion.

We are in complete darkness.

Another shell noses its shrieking way into the trench near the entrance and explodes. The dugout is lit by a blinding red flash. Part of the earthen stairway caves in.

Shellfire!

In the blackness the rigging and thudding over our heads sounds more malignant, more terrible.

We do not speak.

Each of us feels an icy fear gripping at the heart.

With a shaking hand Cleary strikes a match to light the candle. The small flame begins to spread its yellow light. Grotesque, fluttering shadows creep up the trembling walls.

Another crash directly over our heads!

It is dark again.

Fry speaks querulously:

"Gee, you can't even keep the damned thing lit."

At last the flame sputters and flares up.

Broadbent's face is green.

The bombardment swells, howls, roars.

The force of the detonations causes, the light of the candle to become a steady, rapid flicker. We look like men seen in an ancient, unsteady motion picture.

The fury of the bombardment makes me ill at the stomach.

Broadbent gets up and staggers into a corner of our underground room.

He retches.

Fry starts a conversation.

We each say a few words trying to keep the game alive. But we speak in broken sentences. We leave thoughts unfinished. We can think of only one thing—will the beams in the dugout hold?

We lapse into fearful silences.

We clench our teeth.

It seems as though the fire cannot become more intense. But it becomes a little more rapid—then more rapid. The pounding increases in tempo like a noise in the head of one who is going under an anesthetic. Faster.

The explosions seem as though they are taking place in the dugout itself. The smoke of the explosives fills the room.

Fry breaks the tension.

"The lousy swine," he says. "Why don't they come on over, if they're coming?"

We all speak at once. We punctuate our talk with vile epithets belittling the sexual habits of the enemy. We seem to get relief in this fashion.

In that instant a shell hurtles near the opening over our heads and explodes with a snarling roar. Clods of earth and pieces of the wooden supports come slithering down the stairway.

It is dark again. In the darkness we hear Anderson speak in his singsong voice:

"How do you expect to live through this with all your swearing and taking the Lord's name in vain?"

For once we do not heap abuse and ribaldry on his head. We do not answer.

We sit in the darkness, afraid even to light the candle. It seems as though the enemy artillerymen have taken a dislike to our candle and are intent on blowing it out.

I look up the shattered stairway and see a few stars shining in the sky.

At least we are not buried alive!

The metallic roar continues.

Fry speaks: "If I ever live through this, I'll never swear again, so help me God."

We do not speak, but we feel that we will promise anything to be spared the horror of being buried alive under tons of earth and beams which shiver over our heads with each explosion. Bits of earth from the ceiling begin to fall ...

Suddenly, as quickly as it began, the bombardment stops.

We start to clear up the debris from the bottom of the stairs.

To think we could propitiate a senseless god by abstaining from cursing!

What god is there as mighty as the fury of a bombardment? More terrible than lightning, more cruel, more calculating than an earthquake!

How will we ever be able to go back to peaceful ways again and hear pallid preachers whimper of their puny little gods who can only torment sinners with sulphur, we who have seen a hell that no god, however cruel, would fashion for his most deadly enemies?

Yes, all of us have prayed during the maniac frenzy of a bombardment.

Who can live through the terror-laden minutes of drumfire and not feel his reason slipping, his manhood dissolving?

Selfish, fear-stricken prayers—prayers for safety, prayers for life, prayers for air, for salvation from the death of being buried alive ...

Back home they are praying, too—praying for victory—and that means that we must lie here and rot and tremble forever ...

We clear away the debris and go to the top of the broken stairs.

It is quiet and cool.

*   *   *   *

All night long the artillery to our left up north booms and roars.

A ration carrier comes in with a rumor that the Germans have broken through up in Belgium. We are unmoved by this piece of news. We only speculate how it will affect our futures. The enemy victory does not fill us with either fear or hatred. We are tired.

We lie in the dugout talking. Cleary says that the break-through will cause our withdrawal from this sector and that we will be sent to fill the gap up north.

"... we're bloody shock troops, that's what we are."

"Yeah."

"Whenever the imperials* cave in, up we go."

"The lousy bastards won't fight unless there's a row of Canadian bayonets behind 'em."

"... lookit all the glory yuh get. Canadians saved the day."

"It's beer we want. To hell with the glory."

*English troops.

*　　　　*　　　　*　　　　*

We talk of when the war will end. On nights when there is little doing, this is a good topic of conversation.

"It'll last for at least twenty years."

"They're making sure about reinforcements. They give the Waacs* ten days' leave and ten quid for every kid they get."

"War babies."

"It'll all be over by Christmas."

"Like hell. First they said three months, then six, then a year. It's two years now and it's only started."

"It won't be over until every officer has an MC."

"Why the hell should they want the war to end? They got lots of damn fools like us who'll enlist, and when they stop enlisting they'll drag 'em in."

Anderson speaks up. He is cleaning his rifle in the corner of the dugout:

"The war will end on August the first, nineteen seventeen."

"Got it all figured out, eh?"

"No. But the Lord has figured it out for me. 'And the beast which I saw was like unto a leopard, and his feet were as the feet of a bear, and his mouth as the mouth of a lion.' Now what does that mean?"

"Well, what does it mean?"

"It's all in the Book of Revelation."

"But what does it mean? It sounds like Greek to me."

"The leopard is France, the bear is Russia, and the lion is England."

---

*Women's Army Auxiliary Corps.

"Where's Canada in this deal?"

A sleepy voice from the corner of the dugout answers:

"Canada is under the lion's tail."

Anderson continues:

"'And I saw one of his heads wounded to death; and his deadly wound was healed: and all the world wondered after the beast.' That was the first year of the war. 'And power was given unto him to continue forty and two months.' Now forty-two months is three and a half years and that means that the war ends on the first of August next year."

"Yeah, but do the generals know it, that's what I wanna know."

"Better write 'em a letter about it. They might forget the date."

Anderson lapses into a martyred silence as he always does when we jolly him about his biblical revelations. There is no shellfire now and he is not taken seriously.

The conversation drifts, lags, and rambles on until it reaches the ultimate point of all trench conversations—the discussion of women.

"Well, one night I was with a tart in London and she says—"

*   *   *   *

There is a call for volunteers for a brigade raid. A hundred men are to go over. Some of our section offer themselves, I among them.

There is a rumor that the volunteers will receive ten days' leave either in Paris or London.

We stand in the dugout which is battalion headquarters. We feel quite important. The colonel is giving us last instructions.

We are to destroy the enemy's trenches and we are to bring back prisoners. We are to have a two-minute preliminary bombardment in order to smash the enemy wire and to keep the sentries' heads down. We are to rush the trenches as soon as the fire lifts and drop depth charges into dugouts. At the end of five minutes red flares will be lit on our parapets. This will be the signal that it is time to return and will show us the direction.

The raid is to take place shortly after midnight.

We are each given a sizable shot of rum and sent back to company headquarters.

At midnight we start on the way up to the front line. We each carry a pocketful of ammunition, a few Mills grenades, and our rifles.

All our letters, pay books, and other means of identification are left behind.

I have left my papers with Cleary.

The rum has made me carefree and reckless. I feel fine.

    *   *   *   *

We are lying out in front of our wire, waiting for the signal to leap up. It is quiet. Now and then a white Very light sizzles into the air and illuminates the field as though it were daytime.

We lie perfectly still.

Over in the German lines we hear voices—they are about fifty yards from where we now lie.

I look at the phosphorescent lights on the face of my watch.

Two minutes to go.

MacLeod, the officer in charge of the raiding party, crawls over to where we lie and gives us a last warning.

"Remember," he whispers, "red flares on our parapets is the signal to come back ..."

In that instant the sky behind us is stabbed with a thousand flashes of flame.

The earth shakes.

The air hisses, whistles, screams over our heads.

They are firing right into the trenches in front of us.

Clouds of earth leap into the air.

The barrage lasts a minute and then lifts to cut off the enemy's front line from his supports.

In that moment we spring up.

We fire as we run.

The enemy has not had time to get back on his firing-steps. There is no reply to our fire.

We race on.

Fifty yards—forty yards—thirty yards!

My brain is unnaturally cool. I think to myself: This is a raid, you ought to be excited and nervous. But I am calm.

Twenty yards!

I can see the neatly piled sandbags on the enemy parapets.

Our guns are still thundering behind us.

Suddenly yellow, blinding bursts of flame shoot up from the ground in front of us.

Above the howl of the artillery I hear a man scream as he is hit.

Hand grenades!

We race on.

We fire our rifles from the hip as we run.

The grenades cease to bark.

Ten yards!

With a yell we plunge towards the parapets and jump, bayonets first, into the trench.

Two men are in the bay into which we leap. Half a dozen of our men fall upon them and stab them down into a corner.

Very lights soar over the trench, lighting the scene for us.

We separate, looking for prisoners and dugouts.

Depth charges are dropped into the underground dwellings and hiding places. The trench shakes with hollow, subterranean detonations.

Somewhere nearby a machine gun comes to life and sweeps over our heads into No Man's Land.

The enemy artillery has sacrificed the front line and is hammering the terrain between their lines and ours.

Green rockets sail into the black sky. It is the German call for help.

The whole front wakes up.

Guns bark, yelp, snarl, roar on all sides of us.

I run down the trench looking for prisoners. Each man is for himself.

I am alone.

I turn the corner of a bay. My bayonet points forward—on guard.

I proceed cautiously.

Something moves in the corner of the bay. It is a German. I recognize the pot-shaped helmet. In that second he twists and reaches for his revolver.

I lunge forward, aiming at his stomach. It is a lightning, instinctive movement.

The thrust jerks my body. Something heavy collides with the point of my weapon.

I become insane.

I want to strike again and again. But I cannot. My bayonet does not come clear. I pull, tug, jerk. It does not come out.

I have caught him between his ribs. The bones grip my blade. I cannot withdraw.

Of a sudden I hear him shriek. It sounds far-off as though heard in the moment of waking from a dream.

I have a man at the end of my bayonet, I say to myself.

His shrieks become louder and louder.

We are facing each other—four feet of space separates us.

His eyes are distended; they seem all whites, and look as though they will leap out of their sockets.

There is froth in the corners of his mouth which opens and shuts like that of a fish out of water.

His hands grasp the barrel of my rifle and he joins me in the effort to withdraw. I do not know what to do.

He looks at me piteously.

I put my foot up against his body and try to kick him off. He shrieks into my face.

He will not come off.

I kick him again and again. No use.

His howling unnerves me. I feel I will go insane if I stay in this hole much longer ...

It is too much for me. Suddenly I drop the butt of my rifle. He collapses into the corner of the bay. His hands still grip the barrel. I start to run down the bay.

A few steps and I turn the corner.

I am in the next bay. I am glad I cannot see him. I am bewildered.

Out of the roar of the bombardment I think I hear voices. In a flash I remember that I am unarmed. My rifle—it stands between me and death—and it is in the body of him who lies there trying to pull it out.

I am terrified.

If they come here and find me they will stab me just as I stabbed him—and maybe in the ribs, too.

I run back a few paces but I cannot bring myself to turn the corner of the bay in which he lies. I hear his calls for help. The other voices sound nearer.

I am back in the bay.

He is propped up against his parados. The rifle is in such a position that he cannot move. His neck is limp and he rolls his head over his chest until he sees me.

Behind our lines the guns light the sky with monster dull red flashes. In this flickering light this German and I enact our tragedy.

I move to seize the butt of my rifle. Once more we are face to face. He grabs the barrel with a childish movement which seems to say: You may not take it, it is mine. I push his hands away. I pull again.

My tugging and pulling works the blade in his insides.

Again those horrible shrieks!

I place the butt of the rifle under my arm and turn away, trying to drag the blade out. It will not come.

I think: I can get it out if I unfasten the bayonet from the rifle. But I cannot go through with the plan, for the blade is in up to the hilt and the wound which I have been clumsily mauling is now a gaping hole. I cannot put my hand there.

Suddenly I remember what I must do.

I turn around and pull my breech-lock back. The click sounds sharp and clear.

He stops his screaming. He looks at me, silently now.

He knows what I am going to do.

A white Very light soars over our heads. His helmet has fallen from his head. I see his boyish face. He looks like a Saxon; he is fair and under the light I see white down against green cheeks.

I pull my trigger. There is a loud report. The blade at the end of my rifle snaps in two. He falls into the corner of the bay and rolls over. He lies still.

I am free.

But I am only free to continue the raid. It seems as though I have been in this trench for hours. Where are the red flares? I look towards our lines and see only the flickering orange gun flashes leaping into the black sky.

The air is full of the smoke of high explosives. Through

the murk I see two heads coming out of the ground. It is an entrance to a dugout. The heads are covered with the familiar pot-shaped helmets—we use a more vulgar term to describe them. Apparently this was a dugout our men had overlooked.

I cock my breech-lock and raise the rifle to my shoulder. The first one sees me and throws his hands high into the air.

"*Kamarad—Kamarad,*" he shouts.

His mate does likewise.

Suddenly the sky over in the direction of our lines becomes smudged with a red glow.

The flares! The signal to return!

"Come with me," I shout into their ears. I start to drag them with me. They resist and hold back.

They stand with their backs glued to the side of the trench and look at me with big frightened eyes. They are boys of about seventeen. Their uniforms are too big for them and their thin necks poke up out of enormous collars.

"*Nicht schiessen!—bitte—nicht schiessen!*" the nearest one shouts, stupidly shaking his head.

I reassure him. I search them for weapons and then sling my rifle over my shoulder as an evidence of good faith. We start off down the trench towards a sap which leads out into No Man's Land.

We are back in the bay where he with my bayonet in his ribs lies in the corner. I pass him quickly as though I do not know him.

The one nearest to me throws himself on the dead soldier.

I spring upon him.

The red flares color the sky. It is the signal to return, and here this maniac tries to keep me in this trench forever. I grab him by the slack of his collar and start to tear him away.

He looks up at me with the eyes of a dog and says:

"*Mein Bruder—eine minute—mein Bruder.*"

The red flares grow brighter in the sky over my shoulder.

The other prisoner looks at me with sad eyes and repeats:

"*Ja, ja, das ist sein Bruder.*"

"*Schnell,*" I shout into the kneeling one's ears. He nods and takes a few letters and papers from his brother's pockets and follows me into the sap.

The earth leaps into the air on all sides of us. I point towards our lines and we begin to run. The field is being swept by machine-gun fire.

I do not see any of our men. We are alone.

We run and stumble over stray bits of embedded barbed wire. We pick ourselves up and run again. It is miraculous how we can live, even for a moment, in this fire. A shell explodes about twenty yards from us. The brother falls. We pick him up and carry him into a discarded communication trench that runs from the German lines to ours.

The fire grows fiercer. We can distinguish shells of every caliber. The air begins to snarl and bark over our heads. They are using overhead shrapnel.

We stop and feel in the darkness for a funk-hole or a dugout. We find a hole in the side of the trench and wait there while the storm of living steel rages about us.

It is black inside. The unhurt prisoner pulls a stub of a

candle out of his tunic pocket. I light it; it flickers with the force of the nearby detonations.

The brother hugs his wounded leg and rocks to and fro with pain. We examine him. He has been hit in the calf of his right leg. We take the emergency dressings from our tunics and pour iodine into the open hole of his flesh. He winces and then shrieks as the stuff eats into his tissue. I apply a gauze and his mate starts to bind the wound with bandages.

By signs and with my meager German I make them understand that we will wait here until the force of the barrage abates. I pull out a package of cigarettes and offer them one each. We light up from the candle and sit smoking.

I point to the wounded one's leg and ask him how he feels. He shakes his head and moans:

"*Ach, ach, mein Bruder.*" He points back towards the German lines.

He begins to weep and talk rapidly at the same time. I cannot understand. I can distinguish only two words— "*Bruder*" and "*Mutter.*" The other prisoner nods his head solemnly, affirming what his comrade says:

"*Ja, ja, das ist wahr—das ist sein Bruder, Karl.*"

I sit looking at them silently.

There is nothing to say.

How can I say to this boy that something took us both, his brother and me, and dumped us into a lonely, shrieking hole at night—it armed us with deadly weapons and threw us against each other.

I imagined that I see the happy face of the mother when

she heard that her two boys were to be together. She must have written to the older one, the one that died at the end of my bayonet, to look after his young brother. Take care of each other and comfort one another, she wrote, I am sure.

Who can comfort whom in war? Who can care for us, we who are set loose at each other and tear at each other's entrails with silent gleaming bayonets?

I want to tell these boys what I think, but the gulf of language separates us.

We sit silently, waiting for the storm of steel to die down.

The wounded one's cigarette goes out. I move the candle towards his mouth. He puts his thin hand to mine to steady it. The cigarette is lit. He looks into my eyes with that same doggish look and pats my hand in gratitude.

"*Du bist ein guter Soldat,*" he says, his eyes filling with tears. I pat his shoulder.

With his hand he describes a circle. The motion takes in his trenches and ours, the thundering artillery, the funk-hole, everything. In a little-boy voice he says:

"*Ach, es ist schrecklich—schrecklich ...*"

* * * *

The explosions die down.

We decide to move.

I motion to them that we are to go forward.

We crawl out of the dugout.

We support Karl's brother, one on each side of him.

There is no shellfire here. To the rear they are shelling our artillery batteries, but here there is only a steady sweep of machine-gun fire. As we are in the discarded trench we are in no danger.

At last we reach the sap that leads to our trenches.

The sentry challenges us and we are allowed to pass.

Clark is waiting, checking off the names of those who return. He looks with approval at the two prisoners.

I am ordered to take the prisoners down to battalion headquarters.

In the headquarters' dugout there are about fifty men congregated. I am greeted with shouts of approval by the officers. It seems that mine are the only prisoners brought in.

The colonel slaps me on the back.

I ask that the prisoners be treated nicely.

"Of course—of course," says the colonel in a gruff voice.

They are taken into a corner and given some food and rum—to warm them up and make them talk.

One of the men in our company comes up to me and whispers:

"They're talking of giving you an MM."*

I watch the noisy scene quite calmly. The officers and men are flushed with the freely flowing rum. The colonel honors me by calling me to his table and offering me his bottle of whisky. I take a drink.

I am amazed that I do not tremble and shake after the experiences of the night.

They are talking of the casualties of the raid. MacLeod was killed by a grenade as we leaped into the trenches. Forty

*Military Medal.

men are missing out of the hundred who went over.

And over there—?

One of the captains in another company takes the little red and black striped fatigue cap from the head of the wounded prisoner and gives it to me.

I refuse to take it.

"Here," he shouts boisterously, "here, take it and send it home to your mother as a souvenir."

He stuffs the cap into my pocket.

Outside an occasional shell screams over our heads and explodes, shaking the dugout.

The terrific noise is gone.

The raid is over.

Forty men—a young officer—two prisoners and—Karl. I think about this calmly but sadly.

       *   *   *   *

The raiders are excused from duty for the remainder of the term in the line. We are sent back to the reserve dugouts. They are spacious.

The effect of the rum begins to wear off.

I try to sleep.

I cannot.

I am proud of myself. I have been tested and found not wanting.

I lie on my blanket and think of the raid. I feel quietly sure of myself. I went through all that without breaking down.

I feel colder now that the rum no longer acts.

I begin to shiver. I draw my greatcoat over my head.

I begin to shake.

"Cold," I say to myself, "cold."

My hands shake—my whole body. I am trembling all over.

"Fool," I say to myself, "fool; why are you trembling? The raid is over. You are safe. You will get an MM—ten days' leave in London or Paris."

I try to decide where I shall go, to Paris or to London, but the thoughts do not stick.

The image of Karl, he who died on my bayonet, seems to stand before my eyes.

The shaking becomes worse. The movements are those of one who is palsied.

I begin to sob.

I am alone.

I am living through the excitement of the raid all over again; but I cannot relieve myself with action now.

I do not think things now; I feel them.

Who was Karl? Why did I have to kill him?

Forty men lost—why? MacLeod killed—why?

I do not want to lie here. I am frightened at being alone.

I get to my feet and start up the stairs leading to the communication trench. An officer comes stumbling down the stairs. He recognizes me. He sees my frightened eyes.

"Here, here," he says, "what's the matter?—where are you going?"

I mumble something.

He offers me his flask. It is filled with rum. I take a long swig. It burns my insides.

*   *   *   *

I stumble along the trench looking for my section. It is quite dark, there are no lights in the sky. No moon, no stars.

I reach the front line. I recognize faces. My name is called. It is Fry. He grasps my hand and shakes it heartily. His face is serious.

"You did fine, I hear," he says. "They're all talking about it. You're going to get the MM."

"Where's Cleary?" I ask.

"He got it," Fry replies.

"Where? How?" I ask.

"Right over here." He points a finger. "As soon as the barrage started they sent over a couple of heavies. A hunk of shell caved his helmet in. He's down at the MO's dugout."

I dash off down the trench. I begin to cry. Tears stream down my face.

It begins to rain.

The drops fall on my tin helmet, making a ping-pong noise. The water splashes my face. It trickles down the gaping collar of my tunic.

The trench becomes muddy and I slip and flounder in the dark.

The front is quiet. Not a sound rips through the silence.

I see a lone figure looming out of the darkness. It is a company runner. I ask where the medical officer's dugout is. He directs me. I stagger on.

Odor of chemicals. It is the MO's dugout. I stumble down the stairs.

Wounded men are lying all over the earthen floor. The

MO sees me. He is an elderly man. He smiles.

"What is it, son?"

"Cleary—Cleary, 'A' company," I stammer.

"Pal?"

I nod my head.

He puts his arm on my shoulder.

"I'm sorry—he won't live."

I stand still. I say nothing.

"Do you want to see him?"

"Yes," I say at last.

He takes me to a corner and points to a khaki blood-soaked bundle. It is Cleary. His head lies on a small pile of hairy sandbags. His chin rests heavily on his collarbone. His face is a yellowish green. His eyes are closed. The eyelids flutter slightly. Over his right eye, in his forehead, there is a gaping wound out of which thick red blood flows. Part of the jaw is ripped off. He is breathing heavily—half snoring. His face is twisted.

I turn to the doctor.

"Is he conscious?"

He shakes his head.

"No, he's out of it. Knocked out. Bad fracture of the skull. He'll soon pass out."

As we talk Cleary gives a loud snort. His legs and arms convulse and jerk spasmodically.

Then he lies still.

"He's dead."

I explain to the MO that there are some of my papers in

the tunic of the corpse. I ask permission to take them. He nods assent.

I stuff the papers in my pockets and run out into the slippery trench.

I walk back to the dugouts reserved for the survivors of the raiding party. I throw myself down on the blanket. I cannot sleep. I am calm now. It is quiet. I think:

Why was I so terrified when I thought of Karl, the prisoner's brother? Why did I stand frozen as the MO told me that Cleary was dying? Why did tears choke me as I looked at his oozing wound in his head, at his jaw which was half torn away?

Why?

The questions press on my brain—cry aloud for an answer. I toss and turn in my searching. It does not come.

It is better, I say to myself, not to seek for answers. It is better to live like an unreasoning animal.

Ask me no questions—I'll tell you no lies.

At the base a sergeant once told me that all a soldier needed was a strong back and a weak mind.

Better not to ask questions. Better not to ...

Well ... Cleary is dead. Dead with a hole in his head ... with his jaw shot away ...

Maybe he was better off. No more war for him—no more fatigues—no more Clark ...

But why did you feel as though your insides were being forced up through your throat as you saw him die? I say to myself.

No answer.

I had seen other men die. Hundreds, thousands, maybe ...

He was a clerk in an office back home. Maybe if he hadn't died here—like this—he would have married a stenographer in the office in which he worked. He would have had children and maybe he would have been run over by a taxicab.

Or maybe he would have contracted a venereal disease in a Cadieux Street dive and died of paresis. Maybe.

And Karl ...?

Maybe he was a farmer or a mechanic. Who knows?—he could have died in a hundred ways in civilian life.

What is so terrible about the death of one of these boys—about the death of one of us?

I guess it is because we do not want to die—because we hang on so pitifully to life as it slips away. Our lives are stolen—taken from us unawares.

Back home our lives were more or less our own—more or less, there we were factors in what we were doing. But here we are no more factors than was the stripling Isaac whom the hoary, senile Abraham led to the sacrificial block ...

But it is better not to think ...

I pull my coat over my head. I feel warm and drowsy.

At last sleep comes, mercifully ...

Canadians attending to a chum's grave
at the Front, France, October 1916

7

Béthune

Béthune.

A dirty, squat, coal-smudged city.

The black north of France. In the days of peace black with the soot of coal, now blackened with the smoke of war.

On the outskirts of the town is a huge slag heap. The adjacent coal mine is idle—but intact. The city is within range of heavy artillery fire. The countryside around the city is pockmarked with shells. But the mine stands intact. It is a miracle.

Béthune. A few miles behind the Canadian front! A haven of rest for the Canadians—tired and trench-weary.

Béthune with its narrow, grimy streets. Its undersized mining population which walks down the streets with that peculiar stunted walk of human moles. Wine shops, stores, egg and chip joints!

No shells scream into the town.

Airplanes fly harmlessly over it.

The mine building with its shower-baths!

The tolerated brothel!

Yes, Béthune is a haven—a soldiers' haven.

    *   *   *   *

We march towards the city singing our smutty marching songs. Songs laden with humor—gallows humor, the Germans call it. There is something terrifying in the eagerness with which we sing these songs.

A song to forget the horror of the trenches!

A song to forget our dead!

A song to forget the unforgettable!

Our bellies are full. We have rested for a night. It is late afternoon and now we are marching towards Béthune with its wine shops, gambling dives, its safe streets—its *bordels*.

Let the thunder of the artillery boom behind us. We are marching away from it.

Seven hundred men, hard, tough, and war-bitten.

Our feet beat the rhythm for the songs.

Oh, madam, have you a daughter fine, parley voo.
Oh, madam, have you a daughter fine, parley voo.
Oh, madam, have you a daughter fine,
Fit for a soldier up the line,
Hincky, dincky, parley voo.

And then the answer:

Oh, yes, I have a daughter fine,
Fit for a soldier up the line,
Hincky, dincky, parley voo.

Mile after mile the verses are roared out with a half-terrified, half-Rabelaisian boisterousness.

Then the concluding verses.

So the little black bastard he grew and he grew, parley voo.
The little black bastard he grew and he grew, parley voo.
The little black bastard he grew and he grew,
And he learned to love the ladies too,
Hincky, dincky, parley voo.

And a word for the generals:

Oh, the generals have a bloody good time
Fifty miles behind the line.
Hincky, dincky, parley voo.

Left, right, left, right, roar the dirty marching songs:

Oh, wash me in the water
That you washed your dirty daughter,
And I shall be whiter
Than the whitewash on the wall ...

Left, right, left—roar the dirty marching songs.

Tomorrow we may be dead. The world is shot to pieces. Nothing matters. There are no ten commandments. Let 'er go!

*   *   *   *

Anderson complains to the chaplain of the battalion.

"Suppose we were bombed or something. Imagine them

going to meet their God with a dirty marching song on their lips!"

But we continue to sing our songs—shouting and singing down the terror that grips each heart:

Mad'mselle from Armentières, parley voo.
Oh, mad'mselle from Armentières, parley voo.
Mad'mselle from Armentières,
Hadn't been ——ed for forty years.
Hincky, dincky, parley voo.

    *   *   *   *

We are billeted on the outskirts of the town. We are to be inspected by the Chief of Staff and we are busy polishing our green brass buttons and oiling our rifles.

We march for a few kilometers out to a large field south of the town. An army of little French boys stand on the sidelines, watching us as we are drawn up for inspection.

We wait for hours.

No generals.

We shift from foot to foot.

At last a convoy of automobiles comes streaming down the road leading to the field.

The company commanders shout orders.

We draw ourselves up stiffly.

A car swerves onto the parade ground. It comes to a stop.

An orderly dashes out and swings the door open.

A little gray-haired man steps out. His uniform is bedecked with gold and red facings.

"Battalion—present arms!"

Seven hundred rifles are smacked into vertical positions before our staring faces.

Behind us the band bursts into two lines of the national anthem:

Oh, Canada, oh, Canada,
Oh, Canada, we stand on guard for thee ...

The general lifts a tired hand to the visor of his gold-braided cap.

Behind him stands a group of young aides. They languidly survey us as we stand at the salute.

The general starts to walk down the ranks. He is followed by his staff.

We are standing as rigid as though ramrods were shoved up our spines.

We are motionless.

A louse comes to life in one of my armpits. The itch is unbearable. I want to drop my rifle and scratch. I try not to think of it, but the biting of the beast is an inescapable fact. Mind over matter does not work here. To move would mean the orderly room and a few days' loss of pay. I stand still.

The inspection takes but a few minutes. The general gets into his car and drives off.

We are marched back to our billets. On the way back we talk:

" ... a little runt, ain't he?"

"Got a cushy job, too."

"Bet he's got a hundred batmen to shine his leather."

"He's got fifty medals ..."

"Yeah, but he'll never die in a lousy trench like Brownie and them did."

"God, no. Generals die in bed."

"Well, that's a pretty good place to die."

Anderson speaks up:

"Where would we be without generals—"

"Yeah—where?"

Clark shouts an order:

"March at ease!"

That means we may sing:

Oh, the generals have a bloody good time
Fifty miles behind the line.
Hincky, dincky, parley voo.

*   *   *   *

We are marched over for our quarterly bath. There are shower-baths in the mine buildings. It is three months since we have been under hot water. Now we will bathe our lousy, scratched bodies.

But even here water is scarce. We strip and stand waiting for the water to be turned on. Fifteen seconds under the steaming water and then out. We soap ourselves, covering our bodies with a thick lather. Fifteen seconds under the water again for rinsing.

We go naked into another room for our fumigated underwear. In the seams and crotches of the fresh underclothing we see lurking pale lice as large as rice grains.

      *   *   *   *

It is dusk on payday.

In the center of the town, in a red-brick house, is the brothel. The house has six girls on duty all of the time—three for the privates and three for the officers. The officers have a private entrance. But inside, it is said, the girls do not recognize this distinction of military rank.

There are no lights in the town. In the dusk the queue extends for two streets. Three hundred men stand waiting.

The children of the town pass the line silently. Women and their men pass by.

The boys in line joke:

"Hell, you gotta wait in line for everything in war."

The younger soldiers grumble impatiently at the delay, but older ones wait stolidly.

As the night grows darker the queue becomes a long silent line of avid men who stare hungrily at the brightly lit door of the house as it opens every now and then and emits a khaki-clad figure which hurries off into the dark.

The line moves up one pace ...

      *   *   *   *

There are no fatigues for a few days. I walk down the roads at night. It is good to get away from the company for a few hours. Sometimes I sit in a civilian *estaminet* and drink wine and listen to the natives talking. It sounds pleasant to hear words which one does not comprehend. In these native *estaminets* the price of wine is cheaper than in the ones frequented by the soldiers. The French here think that every Canadian soldier is a millionaire. They do not understand why we throw our money away so freely.

It is early evening. The sun has set. The men are sleeping after supper or sitting in the wet canteens, drinking beer. I fill a large pouch with tobacco which has been sent to me from home. I stuff the bowl of my pipe and light up, and set off down one of the roads which lead away from the town.

I walk along puffing at my pipe. Nearby I hear the sound of fowl clucking as they are disturbed in their sleep. A pig grunts somewhere in the twilight.

I pass a peasant cottage. An old man sits at the door. He greets me. I stop. He speaks a little English. We talk.

He sniffs hungrily at the smoke which curls from the bowl of my pipe. Tobacco is scarce with the natives. There is a government monopoly, and most of it is sent to the French soldiers at the front. The natives smoke horrible black stuff, expensive and hard to get.

He holds out a gnarled, brown hand. It is twisted into the pathetic begging gesture.

"*Tabac?*" he asks.

I hesitate. One is not generous in war.

His eyes beseech me. I give him my pouch. He takes a blackened pipe from his pocket and eagerly fills his bowl.

We smoke in silence.

He takes a deep inhalation of the fragrant Virginia tobacco and exhales with deep sighs of satisfaction.

After a while we talk again.

He asks if I like Béthune.

"Yes," I say. "They don't shell it, do they?"

"Do you know, m'sieu, why the Boches do not bombard the city? It is a fortified town. You must surely know?"

I ask why.

"That mine there"—he points towards the slag heap which towers over the fields—"it is owned"—he lowers his voice for no apparent reason—"it is owned by the Germans—so they do not shell it. But my barn here"—he points to a demolished wood barn—"it was shelled last month. Cr-r-r-ung! and a year's work was done in. Their own coal mines they will not destroy, but—"

He breaks off.

"It is better not to talk of such things, eh, m'sieu? It is even better not to think of them?"

He asks me into the house.

Inside we sit and talk. He gives me a glass of white table wine and I offer him half a franc. He takes it.

Presently a girl of about eighteen or so comes into the house. Apparently she has been doing some light chores. She smiles at me. She is dark, like so many of these northerners, and has olive, ruddy cheeks. Her hair is shiny black. As she smiles her eyes wrinkle up and seem to disappear behind her high cheekbones; at the same time the bridge of her nose creases, giving her a tomboyish air.

I ask if they have a spare bed. I do not relish the idea of sleeping in billets tonight. I offer to pay. Her father consents.

I undo my puttees and make myself comfortable. I fill my pipe and sit near the door smoking and talking to the girl. Presently she goes into the corner of the room and talks with her father. I hear them whispering.

I sit and look over the silhouette of the slag heap in the direction of the line. The rumble of the artillery fills the air and the gun flashes color the early night sky. It is nice to sit here and watch it ...

A hand is on my shoulder. It is the girl.

"You please give fader tabac? Canadien have many."

The skin on her nose creases again and her eyes twinkle. She runs her hand up the back of my head.

I cannot refuse her. I give her half the contents of my pouch. She runs to her father with the treasure. He nods to me gratefully from his corner.

I continue to sit and think, watching the flashes in the distant sky.

It grows darker and darker.

It is black.

The lights disappear altogether from the sky.

The rumble ceases.

The night's bombardment is over.

I knock the ashes from my bowl.

The old man is standing beside me.

"Come," he says, "I will show you where to sleep."

He leads me up a narrow stairway and down a little hall.

The house is dark and quiet. No lights are permitted.

He opens a door. It is black inside the room.

"You sleep here," he says.

I walk in. He closes the door.

I fumble in the dark and find a chair. I start to undress. I am tired and the thought of a night in a bed hastens my movements. At last I am undressed. I feel in the darkness for the bed.

I throw myself onto it.

In the dark my hand feels a warm, hard woman's body. I smell peasant odors—earth, manure, sweat ... Her hot breath beats into my face. We do not speak ...

       *   *   *   *

In the morning I sleep late. I dress in a hurry and get into billets late for breakfast. Fry and Broadbent tell me that I am wanted at company headquarters.

My leave has come through!

I rush back to my billets. I hastily pack and get ready to go. I draw my pay. In the evening I start down the line.

There are about twenty-five of us in the cattle car which halts and bumps its way down towards the base. The train creaks and comes to a halt every few miles. It is night but we cannot sleep. We talk and smoke.

"I'm gonna walk into the best restaurant in London and I'm gonna say to the waiter, 'Bring me everything on the menu.'"

"Yeah, you think you can eat a lot. Well, let me tell you that your belly is all shrunk up. Last time I was on leave I got sick that way."

"I'm gonna sleep the whole ten days."

"God, another day and we'll be sleeping in clean sheets ..."

*   *   *   *

Dawn.

We are still in the cattle car. We pass an encampment for war prisoners. The emaciated-looking Germans stand looking, as silent and motionless as owls. One of them waves his hand at us as we ride past. We wave back at them. We throw them cigarettes and cans of bully beef.

At last we arrive at the base. We wait in line for our soup and later are assigned to motor lorries which will take us to the Channel port.

8

London

London.

It is three o'clock in the morning.

We are weary with the long hours of travel. I walk out of the soot-colored ugly Waterloo Station and hail a cab. I give the driver the name of a little hotel.

I am taken up to a room. I ask where the bathroom is. In a few minutes I am scrubbing myself vigorously.

It is five o'clock when I turn in. I stretch myself royally between the cool white sheets. Outside I hear the rumble of early morning traffic. I listen hungrily.

The hollow, echoing sound of horses' hoof beats. The roll of wheels on the macadam. The growl of an omnibus as it passes my window.

I snuggle contentedly under the sheets and fall asleep.

*   *   *   *

It is late afternoon when I awake.

I dress leisurely, soaking in each quiet moment. The room

is peaceful. It is years since I have been alone like this. I polish my boots, shine my buttons, and leave the hotel.

On the steps I light a cigarette and look around me. Nobody notices me. The traffic of the city flows on all sides of me.

It is dusk and the few lights permitted are shaded so as not to be visible from the air. I walk to the corner. A woman passes me and whispers:

"Hello, Canada."

Too early for that.

First I must get a drink and then a bellyful of food.

I walk into a restaurant on Shaftesbury Avenue. I order a meal and a bottle of wine. After the first few mouthfuls I notice that I am not very hungry. That man on the leave train was right. I drink a glass of wine and light a cigarette.

Well, I am happy, anyhow.

The waiter sees the insignia on my shoulders. He is a tall, pale cockney. He hovers over me.

"'Ow is it over there?"

I do not feel like talking.

"Lousy," I reply.

A pretty girl sits opposite me. She leans across the table and asks for a match.

I give her a light.

We walk out of the restaurant together.

Her name is Gladys. We walk along the streets talking and laughing. She is an excellent companion for a soldier on leave. She does not mention the war.

We are in the Strand near Fleet Street.

"Let's have a drink," she says.

"Sure."

"Don't say 'sure,'" she says, "it sounds American. Say 'of course.'"

"But I am an American."

"I don't like Americans."

"All right, then I'm a Canadian."

We walk into the family entrance to a pub and order two doubleheaders of Scotch. We sit and drink and talk.

"Where shall we go tonight?"

"Anywhere you say."

"Do you want to go to the Hippodrome?"

"Yes."

We order another drink. I feel flushed.

We walk out of the public house and into the humming streets.

She puts her arm in mine and we walk up the street. Her body is close to mine. I feel its contours, its firmness. There is an odor of perfume.

"Love me?"

She looks at me with wide-open eyes.

"Yes. I love all the boys." She squeezes my arm. I do not like her answer.

I frown.

She hastens to explain:

"I have enough for you all, poor lads."

My frown breaks a little.

"Now, then, let's not talk of things like that," she says.

The whisky is racing through my veins. I feel boisterous. I swagger. The thought of the trenches does not intrude itself now.

I buy the tickets for the theater. Inside, the performance has started.

On the stage a vulgar-faced comic is prancing up and down the apron of the stage singing. Behind him about fifty girls dressed in gauzy khaki stage uniforms, who look like lewd female Tommies, dance to the tune of the music. Their breasts bob up and down as they dance and sing:

> *Oh, it's a lovely war.*
> *What do we care for eggs and ham*
> *When we have plum and apple jam?*
> *Quick march, right turn.*
> *What do we do with the money we earn?*
> *Oh, oh, oh, it's a lovely war.*

The tempo is quick, the orchestra crashes, the trombones slide, the comic pulls impossible faces.

The audience shrieks with laughter. Gladys laughs until tears roll down her face.

The chorus marches into the wings. A Union Jack comes down at the back of the stage. The audience applauds and cheers.

I feel miserable.

The fat comic—the half-undressed actresses—somehow

make me think of the line. I look about me. There are very few men on leave in the theater. The place is full of smooth-faced civilians. I feel they have no right to laugh at jokes about the war.

I hear Gladys's voice.

"Don't you like it, boy?"

"No, these people have no right to laugh."

"But, silly, they are trying to forget."

"They have no business to forget. They should be made to remember."

The comic on the stage has cracked a joke. The audience goes into spasms of laughter. My voice is drowned out.

Gladys pats my arm.

A jolly-faced rotund civilian in evening dress sitting near me says:

"I say, he's funny, isn't he?"

I stare at him.

He turns to his female companion. I hear him whisper: "Shell-shocked."

I cannot formulate my hatred of these people. My head is fuzzy but I feel that people should not be sitting laughing at jokes about plum and apple jam when boys are dying out in France. They sit here in stiff shirts, their faces and jowls are smooth with daily shaving and dainty cosmetics, their bellies are full, and out there we are being eaten by lice, we are sitting trembling in shivering dugouts ...

Intermission.

I feel blue. The effect of the Scotch has worn off.

"Come on, let's have a drink," Gladys says.

We go to the back of the auditorium and order two drinks. It is a long wait and we have several drinks before the curtain goes up again.

Finally the show ends and we go out into the street.

Swarms of well-dressed men and women stand about in the lobby smoking and talking, waiting for their motor cars. There are many uniforms but they are not uniforms of the line. I see the insignia of the non-combatant units—Ordnance Corps, Army Service Corps, Paymasters. I feel out of place in all this glitter.

"Come on," I say to Gladys, "let's get out of here."

She is angry with me as we walk down the street.

"You're spoiling your leave. Can't you forget the front for the few days you have before you?"

We are back in the pub.

More drinks.

She tells me amusing little bits of her life and I listen.

"... so when he left me I decided I'd stay on in London. I didn't know what to do so I took rooms in Baker Street and made a living that way. But I'm not like other girls ..."

So!

*   *   *   *

Inside of her room a fire burns in the grate.

It is warm and cheery.

She takes off her hat and gloves, and prepares to make tea. The room is furnished with the taste of a woman of her profession. Ah, but it is welcome after two years in the line! I sit on a dainty settee facing the fire.

She comes back with tea and a small bottle of rum.

"Shall I lace it for you?"

I nod. She pours a little rum into the hot tea. We sit back and drink. She nestles up against me and with her free hand she takes off her shoes, then she slips off a stocking. As we talk she slowly undresses. Finally she stands up in only a gauzy slip.

The rum is tingling in every nerve. The fire throws a red glow over her white skin.

She sits on my lap and then jumps up.

"My, but your uniform is rough."

I take a roll of pound notes out of my pocket. I put them on the table close at hand.

"Listen," I say. "I like you. Let me stay here for my ten days."

"I was going to say that to you, but I was afraid you might misunderstand me. Most of my boys spend their whole leave with me. I don't like them running off in the morning. It's a little insulting—" She ends with a little laugh.

The fire crackles on the hearth. The rum sings in my head. The heat of the fire beats on my face. Her slim white body entices me.

Bang! An explosion in the street.

I leap to my feet.

My heart thumps.

She laughs.

"Silly. That's only a motorcycle backfiring. You poor thing! Your face is white."

She puts her hands on my face and looks anxiously at me.

I try to laugh.

*   *   *   *

We lie in bed. From a neighboring clock the hour strikes. It is three o'clock.

One day gone!

Gladys's head lies in the crook of my arm.

"Happy?"

Her body makes a friendly, conscious movement. It is one of the many ways that lovers speak without words.

"Yes," I say in a whisper.

A tear comes to life and rolls down my face. She puts her hands to my eyes and wipes them.

"Then what are you crying about?"

I do not answer.

"You won't be cross if I tell you something?"

I shake my head.

"Promise?"

"I promise."

"I always feel sad when the boys cry in my bed. It makes me feel that it is my fault in some way."

Silence. Then:

"You're not angry because I have mentioned the other ones?"

I shake my head.

Cool hands on my face.

Her silken hair brushes against my cheek.

"Now, now—go to sleep, boy."

The clock booms the quarter-hour. I close my eyes.

*   *   *   *

I wake with the odor of grilled bacon in my nostrils. The curtains in the room are drawn. I do not know what time it is but I am rested. Rested and famished. In another room I hear the sizzling sound of cooking.

Gladys comes into the room. She is dressed in a calico housedress. She smiles at me and says:

"Tea?"

She brings a cup of tea to me and we talk of the plans for the day.

I dress and come into the other room which is a combination dining and sitting room and parlor.

There is a glorious breakfast on the table, grilled bacon, crisp and brown, two fried eggs, a pot of marmalade, a mound of toast, golden yellow and brown, and tea. I fall to.

Gladys looks on approvingly. How well this woman understands what a lonely soldier on leave requires.

"Eat, boy," she says.

She does not call me by name but uses "boy" instead. I like it. In a dozen different ways she makes me happy: a pat on the arm, a run of her hand through my hair.

She is that delightful combination of wife, mother, and courtesan—and I, a common soldier on leave, have her!

I slip into my tunic which by some mystery is now cleaned and pressed, and we go out into the street and walk towards the Park.

*   *   *   *

The days slip by.

It is a week since I have been here with Gladys.

We are at table. She is a capable cook, and delights in showing me that her domestic virtues are as great as her amorous ones. I do not gainsay either.

We are drinking tea and discussing the plans for the evening. I do not like a moment to slip by without doing something. I am restlessly happy.

"I should like to go to Whitechapel this evening," I say.

She looks at me with surprise.

"Why?"

"I've heard so much about it. I want to see it."

"It's not nice there."

"I know, but I want to see more of London than just its music halls, Hyde Park, and its very wonderful pubs."

"But very low people live there, criminals and such things—you will be robbed."

"Well, I don't mind. I am a criminal. Did I ever tell you that I committed murder?"

She looks up with a jerk. Her eyes look at me with suspicion.

"It was some time ago. I came into a place where an enemy of mine was and I stabbed him and ran off," I explain.

Her eyes are wide open. She is horrified. She does not speak.

I laugh and relate that the murder took place in a trench and that my enemy wore a pot-shaped helmet.

Her face glows with a smile.

"You silly boy. I thought you had really murdered someone."

* * * *

Westminster Abbey.

Brown—musty—royal sepulcher.

I am alone.

I walk past statues of dead kings.

I yawn.

As I walk out in the bright sunlit street I heave a sigh of relief. Well, I have been to Westminster Abbey. It is a duty.

As I come out, an Anglican curate sees my listless face.

It is wartime and no introductions are necessary.

"Hello."

"Hello."

"You look tired."

"Yes."

"On leave?"

"Yes. Going back tomorrow."

"Itching to get back, I'll wager."

"I'll be itching after I get back."

He laughs. He is the type known as a fighting parson—very athletic and boisterous.

"Ha, ha, that *is* a good one—you'll be itching *after* you get back. I must remember that one."

He asks if I will have tea with him at a nearby tea room. The mustiness of the Abbey has dulled my wits and I can think of no ready excuse, so I accept.

We are seated at the table. He asks me innumerable questions about the war.

Isn't the spirit of the men simply splendid? Sobered every

one up. West End nuts who never took a single thing seriously leading their men into machine-gun fire armed only with walking sticks.

I remark that this is bad military procedure and add that it sounds like a newspaper story.

"Absolutely authentic, dear boy; a friend of mine came back and told me he saw it with his own eyes. Here, have a cigarette." I take one. I sit and smoke and listen to his views on the war. I am ill at ease and want to get back to Gladys.

He talks on.

"... but the best thing about the war, to my way of thinking, is that it has brought out the most heroic qualities in the common people, positively noble qualities ..."

He goes on and on.

I feel that it would be useless to tell him of Brownie, of how Karl died, of the snarling fighting among our own men over a crust of bread ...

I offer to pay for the tea. He protests.

"No, no, by Jove, nothing too good for a soldier on leave—this is mine."

We part at the corner of the street.

"Goodbye."

"Goodbye, good luck, and God bless you, old man."

I hurry back to Gladys. Tonight is our last night together.

*   *   *   *

Morning.

The last day.

I am to leave Waterloo Station at noon. I have slept late.

Gladys and I eat breakfast in silence. She is sad that I must go, of that there is no doubt. As I pack my things she brings a parcel to me which contains food, a bottle of whisky, and cigarettes. I kiss her lightly as a gesture of thanks; she clings to me and hides her face from me.

Well, these things come to an end sooner or later ...

We are at the station. The waiting room is crowded with soldiers coming to London on leave. I envy them.

I say goodbye to Gladys. She puts her arms around me. I feel her body being jerked by sobs. I kiss her passionately. She is all the things I have longed for in the long months in the trenches—and now I must go.

Her eyes are red and wet with tears. Her nose is red.

She looks up to me pathetically with weepy eyes.

"Have you been happy, boy?"

I think of the beautiful hours we have spent together and I nod.

Crowds mill on both sides of us. We are jostled.

I do not know how to go. I decide to be abrupt.

"Well, I think I'll have to be going."

Once more we embrace. She holds me tightly. I feel tears springing to my eyes. I lift her face to mine and kiss her wet eyes.

I run through the gate.

I look back.

She waves a crumpled handkerchief at me.

I wave my hand.

I climb into the carriage.

The train begins to move ...

The Battlefield after a Canadian Charge,
France, October 1916

9

Over the Top

Back at the front.

I find the battalion a few miles behind the reserve lines. They have just had a short rest. We are getting ready to move. There is intense excitement everywhere and of course innumerable rumors. We are going to the south of France, to a quiet front for a real rest—we are going north to Belgium— there is to be a terrific offensive, we are to be shock troops— and so on. The air is thick with these rumors—latrine rumors we call them.

A batch of unused recruits have come up, which gives us reason to believe that we are not going out on rest. The recruits look with amazement at the feverish preparations, they get in our way, ask foolish questions, and make nuisances of themselves generally.

The artillery roar up front swells as night falls.

It is dark when the battalion is ready. We fall in outside of our billets and march out of the little deserted, shell-torn village.

We march all night. Ten minutes' rest every hour. The road is jammed with clanging artillery. There is a steady stream going our way.

Yes, we are going into action; of that there can be no doubt. The rumors of an offensive these past months have not been idle ones.

It is autumn. We are wearing our greatcoats and the hours of marching leave us wet with sweat. We cease talking among ourselves. Breath is valuable. The packs tug at our shoulders. The accouterments bang and clank against each other.

Men begin to fall out of the ranks.

The road becomes rougher. Shell holes everywhere. Gaps in the marching column grow wider. Clark runs up and down his company shouting orders.

"Close up those goddamned gaps."

We run, painfully breaking the rhythm of the march.

It is dark. Up ahead of us we see white lights shooting above the horizon. Very lights! We are getting nearer to the line.

We pass through a charred, ruined village. Guns come to life on both sides of the road. Heavy artillery. From behind skeletons of houses the mouths of the guns shoot tongues of red flame into the night. The detonations startle us with their suddenness. We march on.

Renaud, an undersized French Canadian recruit, marches by my side. He came up on the train with me when I returned from leave and has attached himself to me. He complains that he has a pain in his side. It is a miracle how he can stagger along under his load. I do not know how he ever passed the doctor.

His knees sag. In the dark I see his pale face, it is twisted with pain.

"It hurts me here," he says, putting his hand to his left side near the groin.

"If it gets worse, fall out," I say.

It is long after midnight. We have been marching for nearly six hours. We lie alongside the road for our ten-minute rest.

Up ahead of us a bombardment is going on. A road is being shelled with overhead shrapnel. We see the red bursts in the air. We do not speak to each other.

Renaud whimpers.

"I cannot go on. I have a pain here."

Clark passes us as we rest.

"I will have to fall out, sir," the recruit says.

Clark turns on him with a cold smile.

"Cold feet, eh," he says, and he walks on.

It is time to fall in. Renaud cannot get to his feet. Clark walks over to him.

"Fall in there, you," he orders.

The recruit begins to cry. The company is drawn up, waiting. Renaud does not move. He lies by the edge of the road with his hand pressed to his side. Clark stands over the prostrate recruit.

"Get up!"

The recruit does not move. The officer takes him by the scruff of the neck and hauls him to his feet.

"You yellow-livered little bastard. Fall in."

Renaud hobbles to his place. We begin our march ...

*   *   *   *

All night long the guns blaze and storm. We sit in the damp dugouts and wait for the order to move forward. The recruits are frightened. They sit among themselves and talk in whispers.

We have been told that we are going over the top in a few days. There are no fatigues. We wait and sleep.

I am lying in a corner half asleep on a pile of sandbags. I feel someone tugging at my left breast pocket. I push the intruder away with a sleepy movement of my hand. I doze again. Once more he tugs. I wake up fully.

It is a rat gnawing at my pocket in which I have some biscuits. I sit up and it retreats a little. I look at it and it bares its teeth. I reach for my rifle. It dashes into a hole.

*   *   *   *

In the front line.

It is midnight.

We are to go over at five.

It is jet black.

The enemy is nervous tonight.

He keeps hammering at our line with heavy artillery.

The rum comes up and our lieutenant rations it out.

We stand in the trenches receiving last-minute orders. Zero hour is five o'clock sharp. We synchronize our watches.

The hours drag.

Suddenly our guns in the rear open up.

The German line becomes alive with red shell bursts.

The fury of our cannons grows wilder and wilder.

Firework signals leap into the air behind the German trenches.

The guns maul each other's lines.

Machine guns sweep No Man's Land.

We crouch in the corner of the bay waiting ...

The bombardment swells and seethes. The air overhead whistles, drones, and shrieks.

We are smashing their lines and batteries. The reply is weak. Their guns are nearly silenced.

As far as one can see to the left and right the night flickers with gun flashes.

Renaud comes to my side. His face is white. He asks a question:

"When do we go over?" His voice is trembling.

I look at my watch.

"Ten minutes," I say. I am sorry for him. I ask him to stay with me during the attack. He moves closer to me.

Fry, Broadbent, and Anderson are in the one bay with us. We prop the jumping-off ladder against the parapet.

Five minutes!

The intensity of the bombardment seems to have reached its peak. The trench shivers with the force of the blasting.

Fry comes to my side. He holds his hand out.

"So long," he says. "I won't come out of this."

"Don't be crazy."

"Yes, I'm going to get it this time." His lips are stretched tight over his teeth. "And I don't care, either. I'm fed up."

He holds the Lewis gun ready to throw it up over the parapet.

Suddenly No Man's Land becomes a curtain of fire. A million shells seem to explode out there. Smoke curls heavenwards. The fierce flicker is blinding.

Barrage!

We are to advance behind the sheet of secthing flame.

I look at Renaud. His eyes are wide open. He keeps licking his parched lips. I shout a few last warnings into his ear. "Don't run. Keep well behind the barrage. If you run into it you'll be torn to pieces."

Clark comes into the bay. He looks at his watch. He shouts something. We do not hear what he shouts but we know it is the order to go over.

We clamber up the ladder and out onto the field.

All along the line men are advancing with their rifles on guard.

We walk slowly. The curtain of fire moves on, methodically.

Out of the smoke behind us tanks crawl like huge beetles spitting fire. They pass us. From one of the holes a hand waves to us.

On and on!

We walk behind the raging curtain of flame. The earth trembles and shakes as though it was tortured by an earthquake. Our steps are unsteady.

We have advanced about a hundred yards.

There is no enemy fire.

It is nearly dawn. A blue-gray light appears.

Renaud walks by my side. His face is red with excitement now. To my left Anderson and Fry walk together.

We reach the German front line.

It is pulverized.

Legs and arms in gray rags lie here and there. The trenches are almost flattened.

In the smoke-murk I step on something. It is soft. I look down. It is the ripped-open stomach of a German.

We walk on. The shield of fire advances.

Through the haze of smoke we see a wood about a hundred yards ahead of us. The barrage leaps upon it. Torn trunks of trees fly into the air. Large branches fall near us. We dodge them.

We are in the wood.

We advance cautiously for fear of snipers.

There is a movement in one of the trees which has remained standing. Broadbent raises his rifle to his shoulder and shoots into the shattered branches.

A rifle drops—and then the man. He holds his shoulder from whence comes a thin trickle of blood. The rifle is fitted with telescopic sights.

A sniper!

Some of our boys rush to him and cover him with their rifles. The wounded sniper crawls on his knees towards us. He is middle-aged and has a gray walrus mustache—fatherly-looking. His hands are folded in the gesture which pleads for pity.

"*Drei Kinder*—three children," he shrieks.

We are on top of him.

Broadbent runs his bayonet into the kneeling one's throat. The body collapses.

Some of us kick at the prostrate body as we pass it. It quivers a little with each kick.

It begins to rain.

It pours. Sheets of it.

Up in the sky we see flashes of lightning, but we cannot hear the thunder for the roar of the artillery.

The earth is pulverized from the heavy bombardment and this mixes with the rain, soon making a thin half-liquid mud. It is ankle-deep. We flounder and slip and fall as we walk.

The barrage lifts.

We run through the mud slowly. It holds our boots. We slip and stagger. We are covered with mud. We can hear the thunder now; it is tame after the barrage.

Machine guns hammer at us.

Men begin to fall.

Shells explode out in front, showering us with slime.

We are held up.

The field has become a sea of mud.

Our light artillery is coming up behind us. The drivers are lashing at the horses. The mud is almost knee-deep. The wheels stick. The rain pours down upon us ceaselessly.

Near me a driver dismounts and grabs hold of the reins and tries to pull his horses out of the mud. The beasts struggle and hold back. He strikes the animal nearest to him with the stock of his whip. He beats its face. Blood spurts from the animal's nose. It screams. The heavy steel guns sink lower into the mud.

Each step is agony. The mud sucks us down. But we keep going nevertheless.

Grenades land in the mud and do not explode.

We are near their trenches. With a superhuman effort we run towards them. We can see the enemy leaving his positions and fleeing to the rear. We slide out of the mud of the field into the half-water-filled trenches.

We have gained our objective.

We start to bail the water out of the trench. We repair the parapets. Our saturated clothes hang on us like leaden garments.

I look at my watch. It is six o'clock.

One hour to cross that field!

      *   *   *   *

The rain stops. It is quiet.

We open our haversacks and start to eat.

At noon they begin to shell our line. The fire is weak. It lasts about ten minutes.

Suddenly it stops.

Counterattack!

We put the Lewis gun on the parapet. Broadbent works it while Anderson stands by feeding him ammunition.

The Germans run slowly across the muddy field towards us. There are swarms of them. I fire my rifle point-blank into the slow-moving ranks.

They keep coming.

To my right the Lewis gun leaps and tugs as though it were a living thing.

When they are about fifty yards from us they break and run back to their lines again. We continue to fire until we cannot see them any longer.

It is quiet save for the swishing sound of the rain which has started again.

In front of our lines we can hear their wounded calling for help. They moan and howl.

We settle down to rest.

Suddenly machine-gun fire opens up. We jump to the parapets.

They are coming again!

They advance in waves, in close formation. We stand on the firing-step and shoot into the closely packed ranks. Every shot tells. My rifle is hot. On all sides of us machine guns hammer at the attacking ranks.

They are insane, it seems.

We cannot miss them.

On and on they come.

Above the clatter of the Lewis guns I can hear snatches of song. They are singing.

They are close to us. I fire carefully.

They are close enough to throw grenades.

I see their ranks waver for a moment and then they start to run slowly towards us. Our line is a line of flame. Every gun is in action.

The singing is quite distinct now.

I can see faces clearly.

Each burst of Broadbent's gun cuts a swath in the front ranks of the attacking troops.

They are close to our trenches. Their singing has become a shriek which we hear above the hammering of our rifles and guns.

I am filled with a frenzied hatred for these men. They want to kill me but I will stay here and shoot at them until I am either shot or stabbed down. I grit my teeth. We are snarling, savage beasts.

Their dead and wounded are piled up about four deep.

They climb over them as they advance.

Suddenly they break and retreat.

We have repulsed them again. Their wounded crawl towards our trenches. We shoot at them.

The shrieking and howling out in front of us sounds like a madhouse in turmoil.

We sink down to the bottom of our trenches exhausted.

It is quiet once more.

Out in front the wounded men still howl. One of them crawls into our trench and falls near us. Half of his face is shot away.

His breath smells of ether! No wonder they attacked like madmen!

Fry has a flesh wound in his right arm. We dress the wound. It is not serious and we advise him to go back as soon as it is dark.

Out in front the cries of the wounded are worse than ever. We look at each other with drawn, frightened faces.

*   *   *   *

The afternoon wears on. We busy ourselves with repairing the trench. We dig it deeper and sandbag our parapets. Behind the German lines we hear them preparing for another attack. We hear voices, commands.

It is nearly dusk.

They begin to shell our trench. They have not got the correct range and the shells fall short in No Man's Land. The shells leap among the bodies of the wounded and dead. The lashing of the bombardment starts them shrieking again. It hurls torn limbs and entrails into our trench.

*   *   *   *

We are lost.

Our ammunition is short.

Fry comes into our bay. His arm is stiff, he cannot move it.

We talk of retreating. We work out a plan for falling back.

Anderson begins to pray in a subdued, scared voice:

"O Lord, look down upon me. Search me out in Thine infinite pity ..."

Broadbent turns on him in disgust.

"For the Lord's sake, Anderson, don't tell God where you are or we'll all get killed. Stop whining."

The shells come closer and closer.

We decide to fall back if the coming counterattack threatens to be successful.

The fire lifts.

We "stand to."

We place the Lewis gun on the parapet and begin to sweep the field. Anderson is working the gun. Broadbent supplies him with freshly filled pans of ammunition.

Across the field we see them climbing out of their trenches. At last our artillery comes to life. Overhead shrapnel hisses over our heads and cracks to fragments in the face of the attacking Germans.

Still they come. The field is full of them. We see their officers out in front of them. Bullets whiz past our heads and smack against the parados in the rear. The firing grows fiercer.

They are about a hundred yards from us. At a given moment they fling themselves down. In that moment their artillery begins to hammer at our trench. They have the range now. The shells scream and whistle and crash into the trenches, on the parapets, behind us, on all sides of us.

We cower down. We cannot face the fire.

The trench begins to cave in.

Sandbags are blown into the air.

The trench is nearly flattened.

The shelling lifts and passes to the rear.

Out in front we hear a maddened howl.

They are coming!

We look behind us. They have laid down a barrage to cut us off.

We are doomed.

Anderson jumps from his gun and lies groveling in the bottom of the shallow trench. I tell Renaud to keep firing his rifle from the corner of the bay. Broadbent takes the gun and I stand by feeding him with what ammunition we have left.

They are close to us now.

They are hurling hand grenades.

Broadbent sweeps his gun but still they come.

The field in front is smothered with gray smoke.

I hear a long-drawn-out hiss.

Ssss-s-sss!

I look to my right from where the sound comes. A stream of flame is shooting into the trench.

Flamenwerfer! Flame-throwers!

In the front rank of the attackers a man is carrying a square tank strapped to his back. A jet of flame comes from a nozzle which he holds in his hand. There is an odor of chemicals.

Broadbent shrieks in my ear:

"Get that bastard with the flame."

I take my rifle and start to fire. Broadbent sweeps the gun in the direction of the flame-thrower also. Anderson looks nervously to the rear.

"Grenades," I shout to him.

He starts to hurl bombs into the ranks of the storm troops.

Odor of burning flesh. It does not smell unpleasant.

I hear a shriek to my right but I cannot turn to see who it is.

We continue to fire towards the flame-thrower. Broadbent puts a fresh pan on the gun. He pulls the trigger. The gun spurts flame. He sprays the flame-thrower. A bullet strikes the tank on his back. There is a hissing explosion. The man disappears in a cloud of flame and smoke.

To my right the shrieking becomes louder.

It is Renaud.

He has been hit by the flame-thrower.

Flame sputters on his clothing. Out of one of his eyes tongues of blue flame flicker. His shrieks are unbearable.

He throws himself into the bottom of the trench and rolls around trying to extinguish the fire. As I look at him his clothing bursts into a sheet of flame. Out of the hissing ball of fire we still hear him screaming.

Broadbent looks at me and then draws his revolver and fires three shots into the flaming head of the recruit.

The advance is held up for a while. The attackers are lying down taking advantage of whatever cover they can find. They are firing at us with machine guns.

We decide to retreat.

I motion to Fry to jump up over the parados. At that moment Clark crawls into the bay. He motions to Fry who is about to crawl over the top of the trench to come down. Fry points to his arm.

"Get the hell down here," Clark shouts.

Fry does not obey but still points to his arm.

Clark draws his revolver. Broadbent steps up to intervene. Clark turns. Fry reaches into his holster with his left hand. He fires at the officer's back. Clark sags to the bottom of the trench with a look of wonder in his face.

It is nearly dark.

Out in front the firing increases. Broadbent goes to the gun and throws a last pan on it. He sweeps across the field. We hop up over the parados and start to run to the rear.

The shells burst all around us.

We are ankle-deep in mud.

On all sides of us men are running back.

Behind us we hear the Germans shriek as they make the final rush for the abandoned trench.

We run slowly. The rain starts to drizzle again. We pass the cadavers of artillery horses. A shower of shells explodes in front of us. We are near the woods again. There we will find shelter from the sledgehammer strokes of the bombardment.

Fry and Anderson run in front, Broadbent and I to the rear.

Behind us the enemy is sweeping at us with his machine guns. With our remaining energy we make a spurt towards the stumps of trees behind which we will find shelter.

A shell lands in front of us.

Fry's legs from the knees down are torn from under him.

He runs a few paces on his gushing stumps and collapses.

As I pass him he entwines my legs with his hands.

"Save me," he screams into my face. "Don't leave me here alone."

I shake him off and run towards the woods with Broadbent.

We run past the mutilated trees and at last find ourselves near our old trench again. An officer calls us into a bay. Other men of our company are there. Broadbent is detailed for sentry duty. I crawl into a dugout and go to sleep.

    *   *   *   *

The sector is a sea of mud. From the rear they have built a "duckboard" road—strips of wood nailed together and laid across a roadway of sandbags.

Down one of these roads what is left of the battalion dribbles down towards the rear. We pass corpses stuck in the mud—walking wounded who became dizzy and fell into the thin black ooze and were drowned.

At last we reach a cobblestone road. It feels good to have something solid under one's feet. We find a refreshment dugout and pile in for cocoa and bread and butter. In the light of the oil lamp we look haggard and worn. Our faces are black with the mud through which the stubble of beards protrudes. We are a ghastly-looking crew.

Our officer, a lieutenant from Company "D," is in charge of us. He calls the roll. Broadbent and I are the only survivors of our section. Anderson got lost somewhere in the woods.

We climb into waiting lorries outside of the shelter. Gears grind. We begin our ride back to rest.

Stretcher bearers and German prisoners bringing in wounded at Vimy Ridge, during the Battle of Vimy Ridge, Vimy Ridge, France, April 1917

10

An Interlude

The lorries stop. We get out. In the dark we fall in and start to march somewhere. We are far from the line. It is nearly dawn.

My boots are twisted and hard after being wet. They cut into my feet. Every step I take shoots a pain up my leg. I limp as I march. The sun comes up and still we keep going.

We pass houses without gaping holes in them. Children peep out from behind half-opened doors and stare at us as we straggle past. Finally we come to a halt in a neat village. The inhabitants rush out to look at us.

There is no shortage of billets. Broadbent and I are quartered together in a real house. No barns or pigsties this time.

The house is occupied by an old woman about seventy, her husband, and two young women.

I limp into the dining room of the cottage. I sink into a chair. I untwist my puttees and take my boots and socks off.

The sock sticks to my bloody foot. It is as raw-looking as an uncooked hamburger steak. The old woman kneels down by my side and takes my foot in her hand.

"My poor one ... my poor one," she says in French.

She gives hurried orders to her gnarled husband and to her daughters. They bring hot water and a basin of olive oil.

She takes my bruised foot and bathes it in the hot water. I wince as she immerses it. It stings. She pours the oil over the raw wound. It is soothing. She wraps my feet in makeshift bandages. In between whiles she tells me that she has two sons in the war. She takes two soiled photographs from a pocket-book and points sadly to the likenesses.

The daughters help me upstairs to a room which the old lady has set aside for me. As I go up the stairs Broadbent grins at me and says: "You sure get all the luck."

The mail for the battalion comes up. Most of the boys to whom packages are addressed are either wounded or killed. We share them among ourselves. Rations are plentiful too. There are no fatigues and wine is cheap here. Madame with whom we are billeted is like a mother to us. We begin to put on flesh.

In the evening we sit listening to her telling us stories of her two boys. The old man sits by and nods his head in agreement. We are becoming quite domesticated.

*   *   *   *

Recruits come up from the base. The battalion is being filled up. New officers are assigned to us. Discipline tightens.

We are taken out every morning now for two hours' drill.

Broadbent is made a sergeant and I am given two chevrons. He jokes with me about my promotion:

"You know what a corporal is?"

"What?"

"A batman for the privates. You get hell from the officers and no rest from your men."

There are new faces on all sides of us. Broadbent and I stick together. We have many things in common ...

We have been in this village more than a month now. At last the order comes that we are to move on. The villagers stand in their doorways and look silently at us as we are drawn up. One of the girls comes out and puts a parcel of food into my hands.

"Company, by the right, quick—march!"

The old lady runs along by the side of my section for a few steps.

She puts her face up to mine and kisses me.

"Remember," she says, "take good care of your feet ..."

The girls and women wave their hands to us. A company of little boys—those serious-faced little boys of northern France—escort us to the outskirts of the village. We turn to the right and swing up towards the line.

Attacking under smoke, France, June 1916

11

Arras

April, 1918.

We are in reserves on a quiet front up north close to the Belgian border. Reports of a German breakthrough reach us. We hear that the enemy is close to Paris. To the south we hear continuous artillery thunder. Our officers give us talks on the need for determination and courage. They tell us that we are not to become panic-stricken. There is no danger.

That night we are relieved and marched towards the rear.

The next morning we are drawn up for parade and addressed by the commander of the division. He tells us that the commander-in-chief has chosen the Canadian corps to act as shock troops to break the German offensive. We are to be a flying column, and wherever the line weakens we are to be rushed in to fill the gap.

"I hope," he concludes, "that you will conduct yourselves to the greater glory of Canadian arms."

The term "Canadian arms" sounds strange to us. Most of

us are clerks, students, farmers, and mechanics—but staff officers have a way of speaking like that. To us this business of military glory and arms means carrying parties, wiring fatigues, wet clothes, and cowering in a trench under shellfire. We stand rigid and listen to the harangue.

We are marched to a road on which an endless line of motor lorries stands. They are enormous five-ton affairs. We pile on. We are crowded in—twenty to a truck. We start towards the south.

We ride all day. As far as we can see the line of black lorries stretches before us. We dash through villages, past forests and lonely farmhouses without a stop. Occasionally we change our direction.

In the afternoon we stop while the lorries are refueled. We look about for the field kitchens. There are none. We are hungry.

The men begin to grumble.

"Hey, when do we eat?"

"How about some grub?"

We are told we will get our rations when we arrive at our destination the next morning. Talk becomes mutinous.

A voice shouts:

"Are we downhearted?"

There is a medley of replies:

"You're goddamned right; we are."

"T'hell with the war."

"We want grub."

We climb into the lorries and the tiresome ride begins again.

Night.

We are still riding. The bumping and bouncing of the lorries has tired us out completely.

The road becomes rougher. There must have been a battle in this vicinity, for the roads are full of fresh, yellow shell holes. It is impossible to lie down to rest; there is little room and the jolting of the truck is almost unbearable. We recline against the fenced sides of the lorry. We have not stopped for hours.

We defecate from between the bars at the side of the bouncing truck—a difficult and unpleasant task.

We stand, sit, or recline in attitudes of hopeless despair. We are hungry, thirsty—we have smoked our last few cigarettes. A light drizzle begins to fall; there is no tarpaulin covering over the top of the truck.

To the left, up towards the line a mile or two away, we see an ammunition dump blowing itself up in sporadic explosions. It must have been hit by a stray shell. In the blackness of the night it looks as though a boy had thrown a match among a giant heap of fireworks. We have seen these things before—they keep on going off for weeks—open-air enormous storage places for ammunition supplies, sometimes a mile square in area.

We crowd to the side of the truck to watch the sight. We talk among ourselves about it.

"They say those 'coalbox' shells cost five thousand dollars each."

"Can you imagine what a little barrage costs, then?"

We lapse into silence as we try to calculate the possible

cost of a preliminary bombardment. After a while someone says in an awed voice:

"Millions, I guess."

"Then what must a scrap like Passchendaele cost? They were hammering away there for months. First the Belgians tried to take it, then the Imperials, then the Anzacs, and then we did. They must've fired millions of shells ..."

This problem in mathematics is too much for us. If one twelve-inch shell costs five thousand dollars, then a major battle must cost—it is too much ...

"I bet that dump going up over there must cost a billion dollars."

"And I'll bet somebody is making a profit on those shells whether they are fired at the Germans or whether they just blow up ..."

"Sure they do."

A surprised voice from a corner says:

"Just think of all the people that's getting a big hunk of swag out of it. Shoes, grub, uniforms, bully beef ..."

He breaks off.

We all join in enumerating the various materials of war on which someone may be making a profit.

"... and big profits, too."

The lorry hits the side of a shell hole and knocks the breath out of us for a while.

We continue the conversation.

"Sure, and I'll bet that *those* people don't want the war to end in a hurry."

"'Course not."

"At Étaples when I was goin' on my leave I heard a *madame* in an *estaminet* say she hoped the war never ended—with her gettin' five francs for a bottle of vinegar what she called *vin blanc*. Why should she?"

"All of us wish the war was over, but believe me, there's plenty that don't."

"… there's those that make the shells, the clothes; them that sell the food, rifles, socks, underwear, ships, boots …"

Others break in:

"Flags, airplanes, artillery …"

"Officers with cushy jobs in Blighty …"

"Paymasters in Millbank …"

"Society dames playing the Florence Nightingale with wounded officers …"

"… these men who are making money on the war have wives and daughters and women …"

"… there must be millions of them …!"

"… and in every country, too. In Germany and France and America …!"

"… and they're all praying to God tonight for the war to last forever while we're riding in this goddamned lorry …"

"… and God must be listening to them. Look how long it's been going on."

The thought of people benefiting from our misery throws us into a melancholy silence.

Broadbent has abstained from joining the conversation. It is a little mutinous in tone and as a sergeant he did not take part. After a while he answers the last speaker.

"Maybe they're making money out of it, but they don't really want it to go on. They don't think of it the way we do. To them, I suppose, it's just—a war."

But the mutinous grumbler will not be downed.

"Yeah, that's it. To them it's only a war but we have to fight it."

From out of the corner of the lorry, a voice—we are strangers to each other since so many recruits have come up—we do not recognize each other's voices—this voice says:

"There's two kinds of people in this world—there's those that like wars and those that fight 'em, pal."

There is a sudden downpour of rain. We are soaked to the skin. The lorry rumbles and bounces on. We are tossed about like quarters of beef on the way to market. We try to rest ...

*   *   *   *

It is still raining in the morning when the lorries come to a stop. We scramble out, eager to stretch our legs. We are stiff with the cold and the wet. We are famished. We look about anxiously for the cook wagons. There are none. The officers explain that our rations did not catch up with us and that we will eat as soon as they arrive.

We are in a deserted village. There is no food to be found anywhere. We are assigned to billets and sit miserably listening to the rain beating down on the roof of the barn in which we are quartered. We search under the straw for food. We find a piece of hard, moldy bread—we share it among ourselves and eat it.

Later in the morning we pile into the lorries again. We start back up north again. We do not try to understand why we are going back. We are simply going.

The day passes without event. We stop several times but still there is no food. Our officers are ashamed to face us and in truth they are little better off than we are.

Night comes.

Still the line of lorries races into the night over shell-pocked roads.

We scrape the linings of our pockets for shreds and crumbs of tobacco, and with this we roll cigarettes in coarse paper. We pass the soggy makeshift cigarettes around from mouth to mouth.

Up towards the front we hear the thunder of the artillery, it rises and falls but never fully subsides. Now and then from various points it breaks out into a rapid tempo.

We stop during the night in a gutted village. Straggling, haggard English troops pour into the streets from the road leading down from the line. They are pale, like us, from the lack of sleep. Many of them are walking wounded.

"How is it up there?" we ask.

"'Orrible. 'Einie 'as come through and no mistake."

We try to cadge some cigarettes, but there are none to be had.

Into the lorries again.

We ride all through the night.

The roads are becoming smoother. Apparently we are going further behind the lines.

We are so exhausted that we begin to doze and nod a little. Feet, legs, arms, rifles, and equipment are jumbled together in the cramped quarters. Every now and then there is a shakeup as someone tries to make himself more comfortable.

"Hey," cries a drowsy voice, "take your foot off my face."

"Aw, take your face off my foot," comes the answer.

*   *   *   *

There is a greenish blur in the sky in the east. It is not quite dawn.

The lorries come to a halt.

Sleepy faces look up to see where we are. We climb down and look about with groggy eyes. My tongue is almost hardened for the want of water. If only we had cigarettes—

No food. Promises. We are doubtful but we have no alternative but to wait.

We line up. The roll is called. The command is given and we march up a gravel road towards the line. Our stomachs are flat through hunger, and our packs tug painfully at our shoulders. Our clothes are still wet with the rain.

The fields on the sides of the road on which we march are freshly plowed, but we do not see a single inhabitant nor any sign of life from the houses which we pass. No smoke from the chimneys. Farm implements stand idle in the fields.

As we march, houses appear more numerous. Soon they line the road. Still no sign of life in any of them. It seems as though a pestilence had swept over this part of the country. We do not see any signs of fighting, not even a solitary shell hole.

Soon we are in cobble-paved streets. We see shops.

No shopkeepers. We look at the signs over the entrances of the stores.

We are in the city of Arras.

It is a large city for northern France. There are hotels, churches, stores, wine shops. It is broad daylight now, but there is not a single soul in sight other than the marching troops. Our heavy footsteps echo down the empty streets.

There is an old-world quaintness about the buildings. We pass a soft brown Gothic cathedral, and in a few minutes are marching past the enormous rococo *Hôtel de Ville*. We look at the signs at the street corners. We read: *Grande Place*. The square is flanked by Flemish houses which are built with their upper stories projecting over the footways and supported by columns so as to form an arcade. Not a civilian soul can be seen.

We halt. We are in one of the main streets. On both sides of the street are stores—grocery stores, tobacco shops, clothing stores, wine shops. In the windows we see displays of food and cigarettes temptingly set out—tins of lobster, glass jars of caviar, tinsel-capped magnums of champagne. I look through a glass window and read: *Veuve Cliquot*—the bottle looks important and inviting. In another window I read: *Smoke De Reszke cigarettes*.

We ask our captain—a fidgety, middle-aged man by the name of Penny—why the town is deserted. He explains that the Germans dropped a few long-range shells into the city a few days ago, and the inhabitants, thinking that Heinie was about to enter, fled, leaving the city as we now see it.

We rest on the curb of the street, looking hungrily at the

food and cigarettes behind the thin glass partitions. Little knots of soldiers gather and talk among themselves.

As I stand talking to Broadbent a man in the company ahead of us idly kicks a cobblestone loose from its bed. He picks it up and crashes it through a wide gleaming shop window. The crash and the sound of the splintering, falling glass stills the hum of conversation. The soldier steps through the window and comes out with a basket full of cigarettes. He tosses packages to his comrades.

Another crash!

More men stream through the gaping windows.

Officers run here and there trying to pacify the men.

As far as I can see, men are hurling stones through windows and clambering in for supplies.

The street is a mass of scurrying soldiers.

Discipline has disappeared.

I step through an open, splintered window and soon come out laden with tins of peas, lobster, caviar, bottles of wine. Broadbent and I visit many shops. In each are crowds of soldiers ransacking shelves, cupboards, cellars. Some of them are chewing food as they pillage.

When we have filled our bags with food, drink, and cigarettes we make off to look for a place to rest.

We climb through a window of a pretentious-looking dwelling. It is deserted. We prowl through the house. In the dining room the table is set for the next meal. There is no sign of disorder—the inhabitants must have fled without preparation of any sort.

We dump our sacks down in the center of the room and begin to prepare the food. In a little while we are tackling lobster salad, small French peas, bread and butter, and washing it down with great gulps of Sauternes. We do not speak, but simply devour the food with wolfish greed.

At last we are sated. We search in the sacks and find tins of choice Turkish cigarettes. We light up, putting our dirty feet on the table, and smoke in luxury.

We hunt through the house and find the owner's room. Water is boiled and soon we are shaved and powdered with the late owner's razor and talcum. We throw ourselves on the valanced beds and fall asleep.

*　　　　　*　　　　　*　　　　　*

We are wakened by the sound of crashing noises downstairs. We descend. A party is going on in the drawing room. Some of our men have found the house. They are drunk. Some sprawl on the old-fashioned brocaded gilt furniture. Some dance with each other.

More men arrive.

One of the recruits, a machine-gunner, draws his revolver from his holster and takes potshots at a row of china plates which line a shelf over the mantelpiece.

His companions upbraid him:

"Hey, cut out that bloody shooting; you're filling the damned room with smoke."

The conversation is boastful and rowdy.

"Some of the men bust into the church and took all the gold and silver ornaments ..."

"... I looked in at headquarters, the officers are havin' a great time too. *Oh, it's a lovely war* ..."

"... There's wine cellars in this town as big as a house. They'll never get the outfit out of here ..."

"They'll send for the MPs ..."

"We'll give 'em what for when they come, don't worry ..."

Broadbent and I go out into the street. It is nearly dark. Men stagger about burdened with bags of loot. They are tipsy. The officers are nowhere to be seen. Up towards the line the sky is beginning to be lit with the early evening's gun flashes.

Over to the south side of the town a red glow colors the sky. Some of our men must have set fire to some houses. As we look we see flames and a shower of sparks leap into the air.

We look at each other in amazement.

"Do you know that this is looting a town?" Broadbent says.

"Of course it is."

"There will be merry hell to pay for this."

We turn into the *Grande Place*. Men lie drunk in the gutters. Others run down the street howling, blind drunk.

There is nothing to do, so we walk into a wine shop. We find a bottle of cognac and drink it between us. We go out again.

The streets are bedlams.

From the houses come sounds of pianos as though they were being played by madmen. Men laugh, sing, brawl.

We find an officer and ask where we are to report. He is a little drunk too. He does not know and staggers on.

The flames of the fire to the south leap higher and higher. Overhead we hear the whirr of motors. Planes are reporting that the city is occupied. Shells begin to scream into the city. The detonations sound louder in the echoing streets.

Falling masonry and bricks make it dangerous to stay out of doors.

The shells come faster and faster.

Bodies begin to litter the streets.

The explosions swell into the steady roar of a bombardment.

The streets are lit with the flashes of the shell bursts.

Buildings take fire.

Men run to shelter. The revelry turns into nightmare.

Broadbent and I find a deep cellar. Over our heads the rafters shiver with the force of the shell bursts.

Other men come streaming down the stairs. The bombardment has sobered them.

Sacks of food and drink are piled into the corners of the cellar.

After a while we fall asleep ...

* * * *

In the morning we awake with champagne hangovers. We feel groggy and thirsty. We go out into the streets. Soldiers are scurrying about carrying sacks of looted provisions.

By noon most of the men are drunk again. Men stagger through the streets waving empty wine bottles. Some of them have found a French quartermaster storehouse where some French officer uniforms were stored. They cut ludicrous figures in the ill-fitting blue tunics.

News of the looting has spread to Army headquarters.

A detachment of mounted English Military Police approach the town.

The police are our traditional enemies.

We organize a volunteer defense corps.

We post ourselves on the roofs of houses which overlook the road which leads into the city. We are armed with rifles, machine guns, hand grenades.

As the police canter close to the town they are met with a burst of rifle fire.

Two horses are hit and rear madly into the air. The MPs draw rein and about-face.

This is our first victory over the police. The retreat is greeted with cheers.

We celebrate the event by going back into the main streets and drinking more wine.

Comrades meet and relate incidents of the day.

"... the officers are as drunk as we are ..."

"... two guys got into a cellar that had one of those big vats ... they turned on the faucet and started to drink out of their mess-tins ... got so drunk that they forgot to turn it off after a while ... when we looked through the trap door this morning they were floating in about five feet of wine ..."

"... God, who would've thought that plain gravel-crushers like us would ever get rich pickins like this ..."

"... the soldier's dream come true, all right, all right ..."

"... hey, the frogs is supposed to be our allies ..."

"What, with *vin rouge* at five francs a bottle?"

"Well, why the hell didn't they bring the grub up ...?"

*   *   *   *

Later in the afternoon the officers appear.

Men are rounded up.

We have had our fill.

Companies are reorganized.

MPs patrol the streets.

Our company is taken to a huge chalk pit on the outskirts of the town.

We get ready to go up the line.

Night comes and we start our trek up towards the front trenches. In our packs we carry tinned goods, bottles of wine, pieces of cheap jewelry. We have discarded our blankets and extra pair of shoes to make way for the loot. We are bleary-eyed and groggy ...

*   *   *   *

The enemy offensive stopped just outside of Arras.

The front is quiet.

We lie in the newly built dugouts and recover from the after-effects of the looting. Many of the men have terrific pains in the stomach. We have eaten too many tins of lobster and other dubious canned ware. There are some cases of ptomaine poisoning. We have no money and we play poker with cans of food, bottles of wine, stolen trinkets as stakes.

There is nothing to do but lie in the dugouts and talk. Once in a while a heavy shell drones on its way to the rear.

"... it's about time this goddamned war ended."

Grunts of approval.

"... first we take one of their lousy trenches and then they take it back. It's a bloody game of see-saw. The ought to call the goddamned thing a draw."

"... what the hell are we fightin' for, anyhow ...?"

"Search me ..."

"Do we wanna fight ...?"

"Quit bellyachin' ..."

"Well, I'm askin' yuh."

"Naw, 'course not. Ast me somethin' easy."

"... and Heinie don't wanna fight either, does he?"

"... and most of the officers don't either ..."

"Sure."

"... and the frogs ..."

"Sure."

"Well, then what the hell do we fight for?"

One of the men begins to sing:

"I wanna go home, I wanna go home,
The bullets they whistle, the cannons they roar—"

"Well, what're you gonna do about it?"

"I say the gravel-crushers on both sides ought to say 't'hell with it,' and start to walk down the communication trenches ..."

Silence greets this unusual proposition. We sit thinking and smoking. After a while someone speaks up:

"Yeah, and what would happen then, eh?"

Another silence. A voice from one of the corners is heard:

"Why, you goddamned fool, the bloody war would be over; that's what would happen."

Broadbent feels that the conversation has gone too far. He feels the responsibility of his three stripes. He intervenes:

"C'mon, there—cut it out—cut it out. This kind of talk ain't gonna get you anywhere. It only makes you feel lousy."

"Listen, pal, we can't feel any lousier than we feel right now."

"Well, it won't do you any good."

We lapse into another silence. Presently the same voice from the corner says:

"God! Imagine all the gravel-crushers on both sides walking down the line. Can yuh see the faces on the MPs?"

He laughs out loud and then:

"Fat chance. If we had any bloody brains we wouldn't be here in the first place."

Like most serious trench conversations, the talk seems fruitless, so we speak of more trivial things ...

*   *   *   *

It is the night of the third day. We are being relieved.

An American battalion comes up. This is their first trip into the line. They talk loudly and light cigarettes. The night is quiet. They call to each other as though no enemy lay in hiding a few hundred yards off.

"Hey, when does the war start?" they shout towards the German lines.

"Oh, boy, wait until Fritzie hears we're here."

We plead with them to speak quietly.

"Aw, t'hell ..."

"Let's get goin'."

"Can the Kaiser."

"For the love of God keep quiet until we get out and then make all the goddamned noise you want to ..."

Flickering matches appear here and there. The shouting continues. We turn our posts over to them and file down the communication trenches. We walk rapidly for we know what will happen if the noise continues.

Overhead we hear the hum of planes.

Finally we reach the road leading to the rear.

"They'll get all the war they want soon enough ..."

Suddenly we hear the roar of bombardment. The front lines are being shelled.

We continue our trek towards the rear.

Stretcher-bearers pass us on the way up to the line.

12

Vengeance

Midsummer, 1918.

We are far behind the lines. No threat of death reaches us here. The countryside blooms. We have been out on rest now for nearly a month. The battalion is built up to battle strength. We drill every morning under the merciless sun.

We hear rumors of battles. The idea persists among us that the Germans will win the war.

We are too far from the line to hear the rumble of the artillery fire.

We start "going over the tapes." White tapes are laid on the ground representing trenches that we will later have to assault. We practice the assault again and again.

We have adopted a new technique of attack. We no longer charge in waves, instead we make short rushes by sections in Indian file. In this fashion each section of six or eight men offers less target to the enemy, only the man in front is visible to the enemy. The section springs to its feet, rushes a few yards, and flings itself down while another section on the flank makes its rush. This is called "infiltration." It is a German tactic. Under the midday sun we leap to our feet again and again and dash towards the imaginary trenches and throw ourselves into the brush or onto the stones and brambles.

*   *   *   *

The company is drawn up ready to be dismissed. Our captain reads an official report on the American attack on Château-Thierry.

"... all ranks are warned of the danger of 'bunching' during an attack. At Château-Thierry our allies, the Americans, advanced towards the enemy lines, and at the first show of resistance, huddled together in groups which offered superb targets for the German artillery. This resulted in unnecessary loss of life altogether out of proportion to the gains made ..."

Discipline becomes more severe. The official automaton salute is insisted upon. After three years in the line we are taken out and taught to salute properly.

We go over the tapes more often.

We go on long route marches.

The food becomes poor.

We are being hardened.

*   *   *   *

It is the first week in August. We are marched over to a neighboring village occupied by brigade headquarters. It is a stifling day. The earth is baked. As we march we kick up clouds of fine dust. Our uniforms are powdered with it. It mixes with our sweat and we streak it across our faces with our hands. When we spit, the spittle drops like little balls of mud. Someone attempts to start a song, but we are too parched.

We rest for a few minutes before entering the village. The usual crowd of little boys is waiting to escort us down the main street.

We fall in and tighten our equipment. The battalion band strikes up and we swing down the cobblestone road past the brigade headquarters. The general stands by the side of the road. "Eyes—right!"

We snap our heads in his direction. The officers salute by hand. From other parts of the village we hear more bands playing.

Finally we draw up, soaked in sweat, in the parade ground on the outskirts of the village. Our faces are as red as the poppies of which the war poets are writing back home. We are burdened down by our packs. Our hot woolen uniforms stick to us and chafe the skin wherever they touch. We form a brigade square—one battalion on each side. We stand erect as though we were driven into the ground like so many fence posts.

The brigadier-general comes into the square. The bugles sound the general's salute.

We present arms. Our bayonets flash in the sunlight. The general acknowledges the salute. We stand at ease.

An aide hands the brigadier-general a paper and he reads to us:

"... and after the *Llandovery Castle* was torpedoed, not a helping hand was offered to our wounded comrades ... no instance of barbarism in the world's history can equal the sinking of this hospital ship ... think of it, more than three hundred wounded Canadians struggling in the choppy waters of the English Channel ..."

The white morning sun shimmers on the general's brass and polished leather as he reads us the report. He speaks calmly and dispassionately, which lends weight and authenticity to his remarks.

"... the lifeboats were sprayed by machine-gun fire as the nurses appealed in vain to the laughing men on the U-boat ... the amputation cases went to the bottom instantly ... they couldn't swim, poor chaps ... the salt water added to their dying agony ..."

Well, we had seen the frenzy of the attackers when they came over reeking with ether. It is easy to believe this story.

The general continues:

"... men, we are going into action in a few days, and we will be given an opportunity to avenge the lives of our murdered comrades ... an enemy like the German—no, I will not call him German—an enemy like the Hun does not merit humane treatment in war ... very well, if they choose to suspend the accepted rules for conducting civilized warfare, by God, two can play at that game ..."

The hard faces of the men harden still more as the story continues.

Other staff officers address us:

"... history will recall that the gallant Canadians did not allow this wanton act of barbarism to go unavenged ..."

A man shuffles uneasily here and there in the ranks.

"... the battle in which we will soon be engaged will be remembered by generations still unborn as the *Battle of Llandovery Castle* ..."

More men shuffle in the ranks. A non-com spits out an order to stand still.

Our colonel speaks out. We like him. He has risen from the ranks.

"... I'm not saying for you not to take prisoners. That's against international rules. All that I'm saying is that if you take any we'll have to feed 'em out of our rations ..."

Some of us laugh at this. Most of us are silent, however.

We march back through that cloud of rolling dust.

*   *   *   *

We move closer to the front. We march by night, footsore and smelling sour of sweat, and sleep like dead men during the blistering August days.

All night long we tramp up the poplar-lined roads. Every now and then we are forced off the gravel onto the fields to make way for the tanks, tractors, and heavy artillery which rolls in a metallic stream towards the trenches.

We are now within range of heavy shellfire. We can see the flashes of the guns up yonder.

At dawn we take refuge in woods or in unused reserve trenches. As the sun rises all life, it seems, is suspended. Neither man nor beast stirs. We are utterly exhausted. The tanks and heavy guns sprawl like sleeping dinosaurs covered with camouflage tarpaulin.

The month of drill and training has made us nervous. We are irritable like overtrained prizefighters. We squabble with each other.

The area behind the lines swarms with troops and artillery. What havoc the enemy could play, if he only knew!

We lie in a wood right behind the heavy artillery lines. It is midday. We are jumpy. Near us a few birds chirp gayly as though no war was in progress. In our maniac fear we think that the birds will give our position away. We curse them:

"Get the hell away from here, you bloody bastards ..."

We sit up bleary-eyed and angry.

We throw stones at them.

They fly away, frightened.

We go back to sleep.

      *   *   *   *

Amiens.

It is night.

We are to go into action tomorrow morning.

We are to take no prisoners. We say this on all sides. It has become an unofficial order. It is an understood thing.

Rumors spread. We are all to have ten days' leave in Paris after the scrap. This is to be the last battle in the war. After this—then home! General Foch is personally taking charge of the advance. And so on.

We hear reports of the artillery preparation which is to precede our attack. There are five lines of artillery on the twenty-mile front standing hub to hub. Shells will explode every second in every three-foot area within Heinie's lines.

One man figures out that a louse will not be able to live through a fire of such intensity.

We sit in the dugout. We cannot sleep.

We talk aimlessly:

"What's the best way of not taking prisoners?" asks a recruit.

There are conflicting opinions.

One is for the use of the bayonet.

"Anyone that would do what those bastards did to the hospital ship ought to get a bayonet. It'd give me plenty of satisfaction, believe me."

"Grenades are good ..."

"Yeah, that's right. Pat him on the back and then slip a bomb in his pocket when he ain't lookin' and then say, *"Raus mit ihm*, Heinie!' He runs about twenty yards and up he goes. I did that to a Fritz at Vimy. He just came apart ..."

"The bayonet makes a messy job of it," Broadbent says. "The guts stick to the blade when you withdraw ..."

A recruit screws his face up, sickened.

"It's the suction that does that," the sergeant explains.

"... a rifle makes a neat job. The bullet is hot when it hits. It sterilizes as it goes through."

One of the latest arrivals, a First Contingent man, speaks up. He has been silent so far.

"Why shouldn't we kill the bastards? Sure, we ought to kill 'em. At Ypres in 1915 I saw one of our officers crucified to a barn door ..."

We look at him with respect. He has a yellow, elongated

face and deep hollow eyes. He looks like a man who has seen terrible things.

"... he had a Heinie bayonet through each hand and one through his feet. Crucified, by God."

The colonel comes into the dugout. He mixes freely with us and jokes:

"Well, boys, we'll have lots of souvenirs tomorrow, eh?"

      *   *   *   *

It is an hour before dawn. It is warm. There is not a sound to hint that this is a battlefield. Nocturnal insects buzz and hum. Birds chirp and sing. We lie hidden in an abandoned field of ripening wheat. We are waiting for zero hour. It is unusually quiet.

From behind the German lines we hear the indistinct, far-away voices of men calling to one another. Hitherto this has been a quiet front and the enemy is unsuspecting.

Far, far behind our lines we hear the dull boom of a twelve-inch gun. Boom!

Half a minute later we hear another hollow report. Boom! These are the signals heralding the approach of the moment of attack.

The third detonation!

Instantaneously the whole world becomes a flickering inferno of howling steel. The roar of the barrage is unbearable. My eardrums ache.

We spring to our feet and advance slowly behind the pulverizing curtain of fire which dances before us. A veritable whining canopy of steel arches over our heads.

Behind us a wave of tanks advance. They soon pass us. We are literally advancing behind a wall of steel.

The air is thick with the pale yellow smoke of high explosives—the color of boarding-house tea.

I feel a warm trickle on the sides of my neck. My ears are bleeding from the force and fury of the detonations.

We advance slowly; sections in Indian file. We walk at a snail-like even gait. Penny advances in front of his company and directs the pace. Sometimes we halt waiting for the barrage to move on out of the range of danger to us. A wave of Penny's hand and we move on.

We reach the front line. It is deserted. The enemy must have anticipated the attack and withdrawn in advance.

The second line is reached and still no resistance. We walk on calmly. The barrage has annihilated everything in its iron-shod march. The trenches are flattened.

The fire lifts.

Out in front we hear the tanks blazing away at the enemy's lines.

The air clears a little.

Out of the thin smoke hazy, silhouetted figures emerge.

"Here they come ..." we shout to each other.

We bring our rifles to our hips, half on guard.

The figures run with funny jerky steps towards us, holding their hands high above their heads.

We open rifle fire as we advance. The silhouettes begin to topple over. It is just like target practice.

We advance.

They come closer.

There are hundreds of them. They are unarmed. They open their mouths wide as though they are shouting something of great importance. The rifle fire drowns out their words. Doubtless they are asking for mercy. We do not heed. We are avenging the sinking of the hospital ship. We continue to fire.

Everything is indistinct in the smoke and it is not easy to pick them off.

They are nearly on top of us. There is a look of amazement in their faces as we shoot. We are firing point-blank now.

The gray figures continue to fall, one by one, until only a handful is left.

They realize they are doomed and they scream. We can hear them now even above the rifle fire, we are so close.

"*Bitte—bitte* (please—please)."

Their voices are shrill. They are mostly youngsters.

They throw themselves into the crater of a shell hole. They cower there. Some of our men walk to the lip of the hole and shoot into the huddled mass of Germans. Clasped hands are held up from out of the funnel-shaped grave. The hands shake eloquently asking for pity. There is none. Our men shoot into the crater. In a few seconds only a squirming mass is left. As I pass the hole I see the lips of a few moving. I turn away.

We continue to advance. Still there is no resistance.

Suddenly the earth in front of us begins to shoot up little fountains of dirt. Rifle fire.

We begin to run. In front of us there is an incline and beyond a ridge.

We run faster.

Penny falls.

We run still faster.

The fire becomes hotter.

Men begin to fall.

Machine guns hammer in front of us. My section throws itself into a shell hole. We wait for the fire to subside. The tanks are out in front of us. We will wait ...

        *   *   *   *

Our colonel crawls into the hole.

"What the hell are you doing here—get out," he shouts, pointing to the ridge ahead of us.

We share the pans of ammunition between us. I carry the Lewis gun. We are dead tired and start to run towards the ridge. On all sides of us men are running with slow, clumsy movements. The machine gun bounces on my shoulder. The ammunition pans clatter against the backs of those who carry them. Each step becomes agony.

At last we reach the foot of the hill.

We start up. It is hard to breathe. It is hot and we drip with sweat. Behind and on top of the hill the machine guns spurt and sweep.

The blood rushes through my head like a thundering torrent. My body is a hammering cauldron of sound. My ears ring, my head buzzes. My heart knocks like a faulty racing-motor piston.

Overhead an occasional shell crashes into fragments, but this is not what holds our eyes glued ahead of us in hypnotic terror. On the top of the ridge little spurts of yellow earth leap up! They have withdrawn from the ridge and are now sweeping it with machine-gun fire. We quicken our pace.

On and on!

Mess-tins and entrenching tools strapped to our backs clang and bang against our buttocks.

Halfway up the hill we slow down. We are weighted down by our burdens. Our movements are like those of one pursued in a nightmare.

On and up!

We are near the top. A few more steps and we will fling ourselves down on the crest of the ridge and get the gun into action. A few more steps!

Our lungs and throats whistle. Our faces are reddish blue with exertion. The veins on our necks stand out like black twisted cords.

On the flanks the ridge is taken. Shells explode everywhere.

The little spurts of yellow earth continue to leap up in front of us as though mischievous boys were throwing stones from behind the hill. But from behind the hill comes the noise as though a thousand riveting machines had gone mad.

We are on top of the ridge. A few more steps to the other side!

I stumble and fall. I jump to my feet and run a few steps. I fall again. I try to get on my feet but my right leg gives way.

My right foot feels numb. I look at it; it is spurting a ruby fountain. The top of the bubbling stream glistens in the sun.

I feel empty inside, nauseous.

I am frightened.

As though speaking to a stranger, I say:

"My God, I am wounded." I look at the blood with surprise.

I roll into a shell hole for safety.

Our guns are hammering into the valley below. They begin to move forward. I lie where I am. The sound of the fighting moves away from me, farther, farther …The enemy is falling back.

I look at my foot. It is still spurting blood—an artery must be cut. Something must be done. I make my handkerchief into a tourniquet and tie it tightly above my ankle. I twist it until my foot feels cold. The blood ceases to spurt and drips now; drip, drip …

I am weak. My mouth is dry and my throat cries for water. I look into my water bottle—it is empty. I remember that I emptied it coming through the biting smoke of the barrage.

I lean against the side of the cone-shaped shell hole and watch the dark red blood ooze out of the hole in my boot onto the yellow earth and sink in.

The noise of the battle sounds fainter and fainter …

I am alone in this hole. Nearby I hear men groaning and howling—I forgot all about the others when I saw the blood leaping from my heavy, dirty boot.

An hour passes. The boot is covered with nearly black

hardened blood. I am wearing a boot of congealed blood, it seems.

Wounded, I say to myself again and again. Wounded—home—no more war now—no more lice—a bed.

I am glad. I look gratefully at the torn boot, at the blood-soaked piece of earth on which it limply rests. I am glad—glad—soon I will see lights coming from houses and hear the voices of women and feel their cool hands on my face.

Yes ... I am happy.

I begin to cry.

A sharp pain shoots up my leg.

I feel in my pockets for a cigarette. Fortunately I have one. I light up and fill my lungs with the soothing smoke. I exhale with a sigh of happy relief. My pain seems less ...

       *   *   *   *

I am thirsty. My mouth is gummy for the lack of saliva. I crawl out of the shell hole, dragging my wounded foot after me. I will find one of the killed and take his water bottle.

I slide into a large shell crater. A man lies huddled at the bottom.

It is Broadbent.

One of his legs hangs by a mere strip of skin and flesh to his thigh. He opens his eyes and smiles weakly. His face is bathed in sweat and pain. His lips move slightly. He is speaking. I put my head close to his and listen.

"I can't look at it—tell me is it off?" he whispers.

I lift his head up and give him a drink of the water I have found. It is lukewarm. He drinks.

At the bottom of the hole there is a wide black pool of blood. His partly amputated leg is twisted at a grotesque angle—suddenly the strip of skin and flesh breaks. The leg moves a little.

"Tell me is it off?"

I cannot answer him.

The pool of blood grows as though it were fed by a subterranean spring. It fills the narrow, conical bottom of the hole. He lies with his face twisted so that he does not see his leg.

"... all the time—you know, in the night when I'd think— this is the thing I was scared of most ..." He moans.

His face is a dirty white—it is turning green. His eyes are half closed. His breathing becomes heavier. The deep whistling intakes sound above all the other sounds of the field.

I move to alter my position. His eyes follow me, beseeching me not to forsake him. I reassure him.

"Is it off—all of it, I mean?" he asks.

"Rest quiet," I say, avoiding his question. "The stretcher-bearers will soon be here."

He looks at my foot and smiles faintly.

"You're lucky. A Blighty. No more fatigues—"

Time passes.

The heavy blistering August sun drags itself higher into the sky. The noise of the battle is a dull rumble now. Midday insects drone sleepily. In the side of the shell hole there is an opening of an anthill. I watch the beady insects scurrying in and out. Two of them struggle to carry a little ball of ordure uphill. Again and again it topples them over. They try again, others come to their aid, and finally it is taken into the dark little hole.

After a long while he speaks again.

"I know it isn't off—I can feel my toe when I wriggle it—it can't be off."

But the leg lies motionless near the pool of blood. He does not look to see, however.

His breath comes faster. He looks up to the globe of fire which seems to hang motionless in the sky. Tears roll down his dirty green cheeks.

"I know it—I'm dying—God—and I'm glad. I don't want to go back—like this ..." He moves his hand listlessly towards his thigh. His face glistens in the sun. "Mother," he whimpers like a child, "mother ..."

Like the hundreds of other men I had seen die, Broadbent dies like a little boy too—weeping, calling for his mother.

Tears cease to stream down his face. He lies perfectly still.

In the rear I hear the stretcher-bearers calling to each other.

    *   *   *   *

The hospital train moves slowly towards Boulogne. It stops here and there to pick up more cargo.

We come to a halt and a bright-faced cockney girl comes into our car. She wears the uniform of a Waac. In one of the berths a man has died during the journey, but this does not deter us from joking with the newcomer. We shout our greetings to the girl.

"... what's the matter with you?"

"I'm sick ... goin' 'ome to Blighty."

"You don't look sick."

"But I am."

"What are you sick of?"

"I've got mumps under the waistcoat."

"Mumps under the ...?"

"I'm goin' t' 'ave a bybie ... ten quid and a long leave ..."

She smiles.

*   *   *   *

We stop at a junction near an officers' hospital. The door of the car is swung open and a man is carried aboard. The orderlies rest the stretcher in the aisle of the car and look for a berth for the newcomer.

He is a young German subaltern. He is pallid with pain. He looks at us coldly as we greet him and does not answer. He turns to one of the orderlies. He speaks perfect English.

"If this is occupied by privates, I ask that I be removed to another car."

The men in the berths hoot and shout:

"Throw the bastard off."

"We don't want the damned swine ..."

"Too good for us, eh, square-head?"

The officer maintains a frozen composure under the barrage of oaths and taunts which assail him. Finally he turns to one of the orderlies.

"Well, are you going to take me to an officers' van?"

The orderly hesitates and says:

"Orders were to bring you in here"—he hesitates and adds—"sir."

The subaltern looks beyond him as though he were an automaton and says:

"I wish to see the commanding officer of the train."

The orderly leaves to find the medical officer in charge.

There is a tense silence in the van. The subaltern lies on his stretcher unconcerned.

In a little while the orderly returns and the German is carried into another van.

From one of the upper berths a voice, choked with hatred, says:

"God—seems like only their bloody privates is Huns—their officers is"—he spits the last word out with disgust—"gentlemen." After a moment he adds: "And we're—we're—" He cannot find the word and lapses into silence.

Another voice says:

"What the hell did you think this was—a privates' war? Listen, brother, all we gotta do is fight it. That's all."

      *   *   *   *

We are lying on our stretchers on the quay at Boulogne, waiting to be carried onto the hospital ship.

We wait for hours.

It is nearly evening.

A light drizzle begins to fall. Under the lights the fine drops of rain sparkle on the gray regulation blankets.

The wound in my foot begins to ache as though it were being probed.

An orderly passes. I ask him for a cigarette. He stops for a moment to talk with me.

"Is it dangerous crossing?" I ask. "They say they torpedo them once in a while—like the *Llandovery Castle*."

"The *Llandovery Castle*?" He laughs contemptuously. "That was bloody murder, brother. Our officers oughta be shot for that. She was carryin' supplies and war material—it's a goddamned shame, that's what I say."

He looks over his shoulder at the looming black outlines of the waiting ship.

"You're lucky," he says, "this one is only carryin' wounded ..."

The *Llandovery Castle*—carrying supplies—war material—I see the general reading us the report of the sinking just before the battle of Amiens—I see the bright sun shimmering on his brass—I hear his cold, dispassionate voice—"couldn't swim, poor chaps—wanton act—must not go unavenged ..."

I remember the funny jerky steps of the prisoners as they came running towards us with their hands held high above their heads—I see the clasped hands lifted over the lip of the shell hole as we fired into it—clasped hands silently asking for pity ...

The orderly's voice breaks in:

"Well—give my regards to Blighty—have one for me."

I am carried up the gangplank.